Learning RStudio for
R Statistical Computing

Learn to effectively perform R development, statistical
analysis, and reporting with the most popular R IDE

Mark P.J. van der Loo

Edwin de Jonge

open source
community experience distilled

BIRMINGHAM - MUMBAI

Learning RStudio for R Statistical Computing

First published: December 2012

Production Reference: 1171212

Published by Packt Publishing Ltd.
Livery Place
35 Livery Street
Birmingham B3 2PB, UK.

ISBN 978-1-78216-060-1

www.packtpub.com

Cover Image by Tarun Singh (tarunsingh@gmx.com)

Credits

Authors
Mark P.J. van der Loo

Edwin de Jonge

Reviewers
Mzabalazo Z. Ngwenya

Yihui Xie

Acquisition Editor
Kartikey Pandey

Commissioning Editor
Meeta Rajani

Technical Editors
Prasad Dalvi

Pooja Pande

Project Coordinator
Esha Thakker

Proofreader
Maria Gould

Indexer
Monica Ajmera Mehta

Production Coordinator
Prachali Bhiwandkar

Cover Work
Prachali Bhiwandkar

About the Authors

Mark P.J. van der Loo obtained his PhD from the Institute for Theoretical Chemistry at the University of Nijmegen (The Netherlands). Since 2007 he has worked at the statistical methodology department of the Dutch official statistics office (Statistics Netherlands). His research interests include automated data cleaning methods and statistical computing. At Statistics Netherlands he is responsible for the local R center of expertise, which supports and educates users on statistical computing with R. Mark has been teaching R for several years and (co)authored a number of R packages that are available via CRAN: editrules, deducorrect, rspa, and extremevalues. A list of publications can be found at www.markvanderloo.eu.

Edwin de Jonge has worked for more than 15 years at the Dutch official statistics office (Statistics Netherlands). Having a background in theoretical and computational solid state physics (MSc.) he started working at the statistical computing department. Currently he works with the statistical methodology department. His research interests include data visualization, data analysis, and statistical computing. He has trained over 150 people in the workshop *Graphical Analysis with R*. Edwin has (co) authored several R packages that are available via CRAN: *tabplot*, *tabplotd3*, *ffbase*, *whisker*, *editrules*, and *deducorrect*.

About the Reviewers

Mzabalazo Z. Ngwenya has worked extensively in the field of consulting and currently works as a biometrician.

Yihui Xie (http://yihui.name) is currently a PhD student in the Department of Statistics, Iowa State University. His research interests include interactive statistical graphics, statistical computing, and reproducible research. He is the author of several R packages such as *animation*, *cranvas*, *formatR*, *Rd2roxygen*, and *knitr*, among which the *animation* package won the 2009 John M. Chambers Statistical Software Award (American Statistical Association). In 2006 he founded the Capital of Statistics (http://cos.name), which has grown into a large online community on statistics in China. He also initiated the first Chinese R conference in 2008 and has been organizing R conferences in China since then. He is a co-author of the book *Reproducible Research with R* (Chapman & Hall), which is under development.

www.PacktPub.com

Support files, eBooks, discount offers and more

You might want to visit www.PacktPub.com for support files and downloads related to your book.

Did you know that Packt offers eBook versions of every book published, with PDF and ePub files available? You can upgrade to the eBook version at www.PacktPub.com and as a print book customer, you are entitled to a discount on the eBook copy. Get in touch with us at service@packtpub.com for more details.

At www.PacktPub.com, you can also read a collection of free technical articles, sign up for a range of free newsletters and receive exclusive discounts and offers on Packt books and eBooks.

http://PacktLib.PacktPub.com

Do you need instant solutions to your IT questions? PacktLib is Packt's online digital book library. Here, you can access, read and search across Packt's entire library of books.

Why Subscribe?

- Fully searchable across every book published by Packt
- Copy and paste, print and bookmark content
- On demand and accessible via web browser

Free Access for Packt account holders

If you have an account with Packt at www.PacktPub.com, you can use this to access PacktLib today and view nine entirely free books. Simply use your login credentials for immediate access.

Table of Contents

Preface

Learning RStudio for R Statistical Computing is a comprehensive guide to the popular open source integrated development environment for R. In six chapters, we will show you how to perform reproducible statistical research with RStudio. The book covers automatic report generating, advanced R code editing, project files management, data visualization, and more.

What this book covers

Chapter 1, Getting Started: We install R and RStudio on Windows, Mac, and Linux and guide you through your first reproducible research project.

Chapter 2, Writing R Scripts and the R Console: A thorough discussion of RStudio's code editing and execution features, both interactively in the console and in scripts.

Chapter 3, Viewing and Plotting Data: RStudio facilitates inspection of R objects and visualization of data. Learn how to create interactive plots with the manipulate package.

Chapter 4, Managing R Projects: This chapter discusses RStudio's project file management features and version control integration. A short introduction to version control is provided as well.

Chapter 5, Generating Reports: Learn how to automatically transform your data analysis into a beautifully laid out HTML page or a PDF report, making it truly reproducible. RStudio offers several ways to generate reports, all of which are discussed thoroughly in this chapter.

Chapter 6, Using RStudio Effectively: This chapter is reserved for R developers who need to get the most out of RStudio—advanced code editing, code navigation, and package development are discussed in this chapter.

What you need for this book

All you need for this book is a reasonably modern computer that allows you to run R and RStudio. This book is not about learning statistics, and although we do not use any advanced statistics in this book, some basic statistical knowledge is assumed. We also expect you to have some experience with R. Although the book is not meant to teach R, some of the less commonly used features of R will be explained in detail where appropriate.

Who this book is for

The book is aimed at R developers and analysts who wish to do R statistical development while taking advantage of RStudio functionality to ease their development efforts. Familiarity with R is assumed. Those who want to get started with R development using RStudio will also find the book useful. Even if you already use R but want to create reproducible statistical analysis projects or extend R with self-written packages, this book shows how to quickly achieve this using RStudio.

Conventions

In this book, you will find a number of styles of text that distinguish between different kinds of information. Here are some examples of these styles, and an explanation of their meaning.

Code words in text are shown as follows: "On the bottom right-hand side it shows the first 25 records of the resulting data.frame."

A block of code is set as follows:

```
meanLength <- mean(abalone$Length)
model <- lm(Whole.weight ~ Length + Sex, data=abalone)
x <- 1:3
cv <- function(x, na.rm=FALSE){
  sd(x, na.rm=na.rm)/mean(x, na.rm=na.rm)
}
```

Any command-line input or output is written as follows:

```
form <- as.formula(paste("Length", "Whole.weight", sep="~"))

plot(x=form, data=abalone)
```

New terms and important words are shown in bold. Words that you see on the screen, in menus or dialog boxes for example, appear in the text like this: "These packages can be updated by clicking on **Check for Updates**".

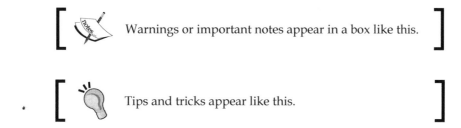

[Warnings or important notes appear in a box like this.]

[Tips and tricks appear like this.]

Reader feedback

Feedback from our readers is always welcome. Let us know what you think about this book—what you liked or may have disliked. Reader feedback is important for us to develop titles that you really get the most out of.

To send us general feedback, simply send an e-mail to feedback@packtpub.com, and mention the book title via the subject of your message.

If there is a topic that you have expertise in and you are interested in either writing or contributing to a book, see our author guide on www.packtpub.com/authors.

Customer support

Now that you are the proud owner of a Packt book, we have a number of things to help you to get the most from your purchase.

Downloading the example code

You can download the example code files for all Packt books you have purchased from your account at http://www.PacktPub.com. If you purchased this book elsewhere, you can visit http://www.PacktPub.com/support and register to have the files e-mailed directly to you.

Some of the examples used in this book use GIT version control. You can download all extensive examples from https://github.com/rstudiobook.

Errata

Although we have taken every care to ensure the accuracy of our content, mistakes do happen. If you find a mistake in one of our books—maybe a mistake in the text or the code—we would be grateful if you would report this to us. By doing so, you can save other readers from frustration and help us improve subsequent versions of this book. If you find any errata, please report them by visiting http://www.packtpub.com/support, selecting your book, clicking on the **errata submission form** link, and entering the details of your errata. Once your errata are verified, your submission will be accepted and the errata will be uploaded on our website, or added to any list of existing errata, under the Errata section of that title. Any existing errata can be viewed by selecting your title from http://www.packtpub.com/support.

Piracy

Piracy of copyright material on the Internet is an ongoing problem across all media. At Packt, we take the protection of our copyright and licenses very seriously. If you come across any illegal copies of our works, in any form, on the Internet, please provide us with the location address or website name immediately so that we can pursue a remedy.

Please contact us at copyright@packtpub.com with a link to the suspected pirated material.

We appreciate your help in protecting our authors, and our ability to bring you valuable content.

Questions

You can contact us at questions@packtpub.com if you are having a problem with any aspect of the book, and we will do our best to address it.

1
Getting Started

This chapter shows how to obtain R and RStudio. An introduction to the concepts of reproducible research will be given. We will first show a simple RStudio session that already results in a simple, fully reproducible report. If you have ever had to analyze data for work, study, or a research project you'd have probably run into a situation where you ended up with a messy kludge of temporary files, scripts, and intermediate results that are almost impossible to untangle. If this sounds familiar, you probably also had to rewrite pieces of your report while debugging your analyses, or when receiving updates of your data sets. Re-running calculations, and re-inserting figures, tables, and results can take a lot of time. Moreover, as a project turns more and more into a spaghetti of files and folders, reproducing exactly what you did becomes harder and harder. Needless to say, things can become even more difficult when collaborating with a number of people on such projects.

RStudio™ is a free and open source tool that makes it easier for you to do the following:

- Work with R and R's graphics interactively
- Organize your code and maintain multiple projects
- Make your research reproducible
- Maintain the packages in your R installation
- Create and share your reports
- Share your code and collaborate with other users

RStudio runs on all the major operating systems, including Windows, Linux, and Mac OS X. Additionally, it can be used to run R on a remote web server. In that case, RStudio's interface will run in your browser.

This book is aimed at beginning and moderate R users who want to get the most out of R and RStudio. In the coming chapters we will cover most of RStudio's features, and emphasize some best practices in statistical data analyses. A few words about R: R is a free software tool for statistical analyses comprised of the R programming language and the R environment. Here, free means not only free of charge (as in free beer) but also free as in freedom. That is, you are allowed to download and use R, inspect or alter its source code, and redistribute it as you like. Note that this freedom is in fact a requirement to perform truly reproducible research, as it allows one, in principle, to check exactly how data is processed in a certain project, down to R's source code itself.

R is distributed via the **Comprehensive R Archive Network**, a network of servers around the world from where you can download R and its extension packages. You can access it via `www.r-project.org`. There are a few other sites offering extension package repositories; the most noteworthy are bioconductor (`www.bioconductor.org`) and the Omega project for statistical computing(`www.omegahat.org`).

The R environment is a so-called `repl`, which stands for a **read-evaluate-print loop**. That is, it offers a text-based interface where you can enter R commands. After a command is entered, the R engine processes it (evaluation) and possibly prints a result to the screen. Alternatively (and more commonly), the commands can be stored in a text file to be run by R.

Users who are accustomed to point-and-click interfaces for using statistical functionality may find the first encounter with such an interface daunting, and to be honest, the learning curve for R can be steep at times. However, in order to make work reproducible, it is unavoidable to store the steps of your analyses as source code. Moreover, being a true programming language makes R a much more versatile and powerful tool than any point-and-click software that only offers a predefined functionality.

Fortunately for us, writing code is nothing new and over the past decades, many good ideas have been developed in the software industry to make coding and code management a lot easier. RStudio implements many of those ideas for R users. Important tips for your maintaining of your R installation are mentioned as follows:

- Always use the latest, stable version. This is the version likely to have the least bugs in the older functionality. You can read about the latest features by reading the news file, for example by running `View(news())` from the R command line. See the *Installing R* section for an easier way to install R.
- Frequently update your installed packages. This is simply done by running the `update.packages()` command from your R console.

RStudio at a glance

Like R, RStudio is a free and open source project. Founded by JJ Allaire, RStudio is also a company that sells services related to their open source product, such as consulting and training.

RStudio is an **Integrated Development Environment (IDE)** for R. The term IDE comes from the software industry and refers to a tool that makes it easy to develop applications in one or more programming languages. Typical IDEs offer tools to easily write and document code, compile and perform tests, and offer integration with a version control tool.

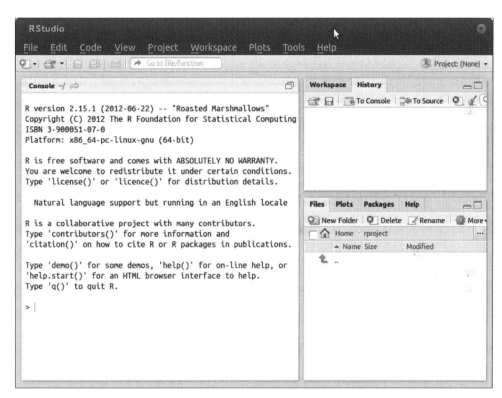

RStudio integrates the R environment, a highly advanced text editor, R's help system, version control, and much more into a single application. RStudio does not perform any statistical operations; it only makes it easier for you to perform such operations with R. Most importantly, RStudio offers many facilities that make working reproducibly a lot easier.

The following table gives an overview of some of the most important features of RStudio that you will learn to use with this book:

Features	Description
Integration of the R console	Type commands directly in the R console within RStudio.
Code execution	Directly execute code from your script file.
Syntax highlighting	Color (possibly self-defined) keywords and functions for easy reading.
Bracket support	Matching brackets are highlighted upon selection. When typing a bracket " [", brace " (", curly brace or single or double quote, Rstudio autocompletes it for you.
Command completion	Press *Tab* halfway while typing a command and RStudio shows a menu of matching R functions. When a function is chosen, its arguments and "help" can be shown as well.
Keyboard shortcuts	Common tasks can be accessed quickly by pressing a key or key combination.
Help integration	RStudio allows for browsing and searching R's native help files, and offers context-related help as well.
Object browser	You can inspect every object defined in the running R session.
History browser	RStudio makes it easy to see what commands you used and re-execute them.
Code navigation	Jump from the use of a function to its definition. Jump from code in a report to the code in the source.
Data viewer	A spreadsheet-like view of tables (`data.frames`).
Data import menus	For some of the most common data types RStudio has a menu that generates the R read command for you.
Graphics integration	Zoom, manipulate, and export graphics interactively.
Project management	Easily switch between several projects.
Version control	RStudio integrates the popular version control systems `git` and `svn`.
Document generation	Generate `pdf`, `html`, or other report formats using `RMarkdown`, `Sweave`, or `knitr` with the push of a button.
Publishing	Publish your reports and scripts online at `Rpubs.com` so that others may learn from your examples.

Readers with some programming experience might wonder why a feature such as debugging support is not in the list. The answer is that it is just not there yet. RStudio is continuously being improved and updated, and according to the forums at RStudio's web pages, support for debugging is certainly on the to-do list of the makers.

Installing RStudio

Before you install RStudio, you need to install R. It is possible to have multiple versions of R installed side by side. RStudio will use the latest version by default, but can be configured to use a different installed version.

Installing R

RStudio needs at least R version 2.11, but we highly recommend you to install the latest version.

Installing R on Windows and Mac OS X

To download and install R, point your browser to www.r-project.org, click on **Download R** (in the text underneath the graphics), and choose a server near where you are. From there, follow the instructions in the **Download and install R** box. Alternatively, use the **Download R!** button at www.inside-R.org. This website automatically offers you the most recent R version fitting your computer and operating system.

Installing R on Linux

Automatic R installation is supported for several popular Linux flavors, including Debian, OpenSuse, and Ubuntu.

For OpenSuse, the default installation can be obtained by pointing your web browser to http://software.opensuse.org/search, search for r-base, and install from there. At the moment, the newest R version is available from there.

The R version offered by the package installer is frozen when the operating system is released. We assume that you are familiar enough with tools such as Synaptic or aptitude in order to install the R version that comes with those operating systems. Here, we provide some details on how to install the latest R version on Ubuntu or Debian.

CRAN hosts Debian and Ubuntu repositories, which are as follows:

1. Add the repository for Ubuntu 12.04 (precise pagnolin) by adding (as root) the following line to your `/etc/apt/sources.list` file:

```
deb http://<your_nearest_cran_mirror>/bin/linux/ubuntu precise/
```

2. Replace `<your_nearest_cran_mirror>` with a server near where you live. A list of mirrors can be found at `http://cran.r-project.org/mirrors.html`. Next, register the security key by typing the following:

```
sudo apt-key adv --keyserver keyserver.ubuntu.com --recv-keys
E084DAB9
```

3. Type the following commands to install the `R.sudo` apt-get update:

```
sudo apt-get install r-base
```

Alternatively you can install the latest R now via Synaptic. For Debian 6.05 (squeeze), the line to add to your `/etc/apt/sources.list` file is deb `http://<your_nearest_cran_mirror>/bin/linux/debian squeeze-cran/`.

The security key is installed with the following command:

```
sudo apt-key adv --keyserver subkeys.pgp.net --recv-keys 381BA480
```

After this, installation proceeds as in Ubuntu.

Building R from source

If you wish, you can download the source code R and compile the executables yourself. This is really only for an expert user, so to paraphrase `r-project.org`: "if you are not sure what compiling means, you most probably do not want to do this".

To make sure that RStudio can talk with the compiled binaries, you need to configure the `Makefile` using the `--enable-R-shlib` flag. So after downloading and unpacking the source tarball, change the directory to `R2.XX.X`, and type the following commands:

```
./configure --enable-R-shlib

make

make install
```

Building R using Windows

Most Windows users will use the default installer, but if you want to you can compile R under Windows. You need to download the latest version of RTools (http://cran.r-project.org/bin/windows/Rtools) and follow the instructions on the Rtools web page.

Installing RStudio

The desktop version of RStudio can be downloaded from http://www.rstudio.com/ide for Windows XP and higher, MacOS X 10.6 or higher, and several Linux flavors. The desktop version of RStudio can be installed easily by clicking on the link for your platform and following the instructions. We strongly recommend that you check www.rstudio.com once in a while for new updates. Alternatively, you can check for updates from RStudio by clicking on **Help | Check for updates**.

Installing RStudio Server

RStudio Server is currently only available for Linux-based systems. Before you install it you need to have R installed, as described in the previous paragraph.

1. Go to http://www.rstudio.com/ide/download/server and follow the instructions there to download and install the RStudio server. Once RStudio is installed, you can run it by typing the following:

   ```
   sudo rstudio-server start
   ```

2. To log on you need to know the server's URL. If you have installed it locally, you can access it by pointing your browser to the following path:

   ```
   http://localhost:8787
   ```

RStudio allows the users of your Linux system to log on with their standard password and username, so user management can be done as in Linux.

Installing R packages

One of the most attractive features of R is the abundance of freely available extension packages. The installation of R comes bundled with many important packages, but newly developed statistical methods come readily available in packages. These packages are published on the **Comprehensive R Archive Network (CRAN)** and can be easily installed in RStudio. To get started, we will install the knitr package, which we'll need in our first session.

One of the tabs in the bottom right-hand side of RStudio is a package panel that allows you to browse the currently installed packages. These packages can be updated by clicking on **Check for Updates**. RStudio will check what packages have newer versions and will give you the option to select which of these packages should be updated. Alternatively you can use the **General** menu's **Tools | Check for Package Updates**.

To install the packages click on the **Packages** tab in the bottom right-hand side panel. Each tab has its own menu items at the top of the panel. Click on the **Install** button to start the installation. The pop-up menu that appears allows you to choose either a CRAN server or a local repository. If you have Internet access, choose a mirror somewhere near you. Next, type the first letters of the package you wish to install. Here, we will install the knitr package. When typing, RStudio will show suggestions of packages with similar names. Choose knitr and hit *Enter*. RStudio generates the command that installs the package, copies it to the console, and executes it.

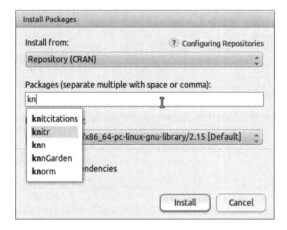

To load the package, scroll down the window with installed packages and check it. The package is now loaded.

 Trying to update a package that is currently loaded may fail. The easiest solution is to close and restart RStudio and update again without the package being loaded.

Overview: A first R session

Now we have R and Rstudio installed we can start our first R session from within RStudio. It is a good practice to use an RStudio project for all your data analysis with R, for reasons we will encounter later in this book.

We create an R project using the menu **Project | New Project**. Choose **New Directory** and name the project file `Abalone`.

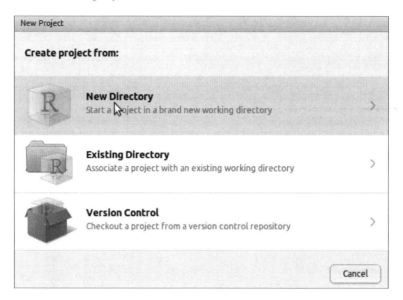

[In this session, we download and manipulate the `abalone` file. This file will be used in examples throughout the book.]

Abalones are a very common type of edible sea snail (sometimes called sea ear) occurring in waters around the world. The data in the file used in this book was compiled and published by *Warwick J. Nash, Tracy L. Sellers, Simon R. Talbot, Andrew J. Cawthorn*, and *Wes B. Ford* in 1994 [*Sea fisheries division Technical Report No. 48 (ISSN 1034-3288)*]. It was generously donated to the UCI machine learning repository in 1995.

If you are a beginner in R programming, the RStudio menus facilitate many R commands. When you click on a menu item, RStudio generates and executes the corresponding R commands in the console window. It is a good (and a reproducible!) practice to put your R code in script files as much as possible; but for now we will use some menu commands.

Select **Workspace | Import DataSet | From Web URL**.

RStudio (and R) can import text files from the disk and over the Internet as well, as shown in the following example:

Type (or paste) the following URL: `http://archive.ics.uci.edu/ml/machine-learning-databases/abalone/abalone.data`.

RStudio downloads the file and shows the **Import Dataset** dialog:

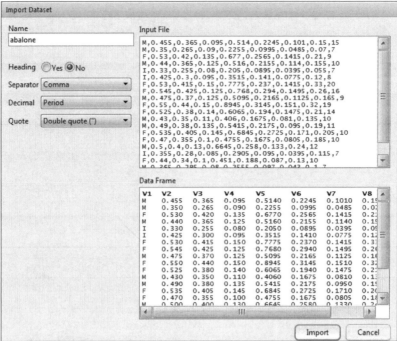

The top left-hand side shows the name (**abalone**) of the resulting data.frame. On the bottom left-hand side are the settings for reading the data file that RStudio deduced from the data file. You can alter these; however, in this example they are fine. On the top right-hand side RStudio shows the first 25 lines of the data file. On the bottom right-hand side it shows the first 25 records of the resulting data.frame. Click on the **Import** button.

RStudio imports the data and creates a data.frame with the name abalone using the R command read.table and the options that you have set in the **Import DataSet** dialog. Also, it automatically runs View(abalone), which shows the data we just imported. Notice that the Workspace panel on the right-hand side now contains the variable abalone. Also, notice that the column names of the data are missing, so we need to add them.

In the console panel we type the following:

```
names(abalone) <- c("Sex","Length","Diameter","Height","Whole weight"
                    ,"Shucked weight","Viscera weight","Shell weight"
                    ,"Rings")
write.csv(abalone, "abalone.csv", row.names=FALSE)
```

This sets the correct names for the data set and stores the data in your project directory, so you don't have to download it again. This data file is part of your compendium.

We will start our first data analysis within RStudio with an R script.

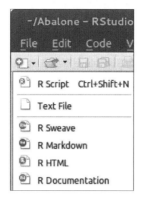

How Start + Store a new R-program

Follow the next few steps in order to start the data analysis:

1. Create a new R script by navigating to **File | New | R script** (*Ctrl+Shift+N* or *Command+Shift+N*) and type the following:

```
abalone <- read.csv("abalone.csv")
table(abalone$Sex)
plot(Length ~ Sex, data=abalone)
```

These commands load the data, calculate the gender frequencies in the data, and plot a box plot of `Length` by `Sex` for `abalone`.

2. Save your R script as `abalone.R` using **File | Save** (*Ctrl+S* or *Command+S*).

3. Execute your R script with *Ctrl+Shift+Enter* or *Command+Shift+Return*.

Et voila! We have run a small R script from within RStudio. Notice that the panel on the bottom right-hand side shows the plot that we have created.

But we can do better than that. If you did not follow the previous instructions to install `knitr`, now is the time to do it after all. You may also install it by typing `install.packages("knitr")` in the console.

1. Choose **File | Compile Notebook**.

2. Close the Abalone project with **Project | Close Project**. Choose **Save**.

   We have now a new empty RStudio session.

3. Open your newly created an Abalone project by navigating to **Project | Recent Projects | Abalone**.

Your environment is restored, including all the commands that you typed, thanks to R and RStudio.

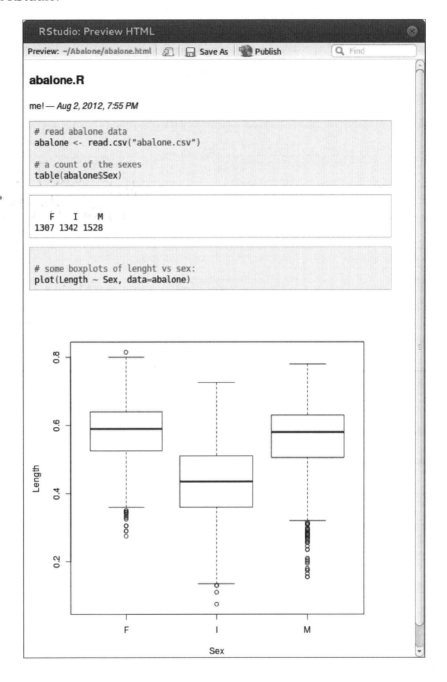

Keyboard shortcuts

Besides the standard keyboard shortcuts that you likely use in everyday computer use (cut-copy-paste, or to undo an activity), RStudio supports many keyboard shortcuts specifically for R code editing, execution, and more. Although you are unlikely to learn or use all of them, it is useful to get used to at least a few. We will highlight a few of the most useful keyboard shortcuts in every chapter.

Panel	Windows & Linux	Mac	Description
Source, console	*Tab* or *Ctrl*+space bar	*Tab* or *Command*+space bar	Command completion.
Source	*Ctrl*+*Enter*	*Command*+*Return*	Run current line or selection.
Source	*Ctrl*+*Shift*+*Enter*	*Command*+*Shift*+*Return*	Source with echo (run whole file).
Any	*Ctrl*+*1*	*Command*+*1*	Move cursor to source editor.
Any	*Ctrl*+*2*	*Command*+*2*	Move cursor to console.

Getting help

If you run into trouble with RStudio, there are several ways to get help online.

Getting online Help w/ RStudio

- The developers of RStudio have shown to be amazingly responsive on the help forum at http://support.rstudio.org/. There are many people using R and RStudio, so chances are that someone has already posted the same question somewhere and had it answered. So, before posting a question, make sure to take a look at the troubleshooting guide at RStudio's support page.

- Search whether your question has been answered before in the FAQs or the forum.

- Google your question. It may have been answered on another Q&A forum, such as stack exchange.

When you post a question, it helps a lot to include a small example that reproduces your problem. Also, you may want to attach the output of R's sessionInfo() command to show in what context the problem occurred. Finally, it can be helpful if you attach RStudio's logfile. You can find the folder where it is stored by opening Help>Diagnostics>Show log files. If RStudio fails to start, you can find it in the following place folder:

Operating systems	Folder paths
Windows XP	`%USERPROFILE%\Local Settings\Application Data\` `RStudio-Desktop\log`
Windows Vista, 7	`%localappdata%\RStudio-Desktop\log`
Linux, Max OS x	`~/.rstudio-desktop/log/`

What if I uninstall RStudio?

Although you may find this hard to believe, this is absolutely no problem. Each RStudio project is just a folder, containing your scripts, reports, and data in their original form. Additionally there is a `.proj` file that holds some session information for RStudio and possibly an `.Rdata` file. So even if you wish to uninstall RStudio, your work is as accessible as before. You can still re-open your last-closed R session by starting the default Rgui and opening the `.Rdata` file in that folder. Scripts are stored as simple text files.

It is important to note that RStudio does not alter the storage format of your data in any way. In contrast, many proprietary products force you to import your data and store it in some binary format that cannot be opened with other products.

Further reading

The paper *Statistical Analyses and Reproducible Research* by *Robert Gentleman* and *Duncan Temple Lang* offers a thorough description of methods for reproducible research. It can be downloaded for free from `http://biostats.bepress.com/bioconductor/paper2/`. There are many books for learning about R, a lot of which are dedicated to specific subjects. Two recent books that discuss R in general that have quickly gained popularity are *R in a Nutshell* by *Joseph Adler*, 2010, O'Reilley, and *The Art of R programming* by *Norman Matloff*, 2011, No Starch Press, Inc. The former book discusses R as a language as well as many statistical features while the latter thoroughly discusses R as a programming language. Two books focusing on general statistics with R are worth mentioning here as well. The first is *Introductory Statistics with R (2nd ed. 2008, Springer)* by *Peter Dalgaard*. The second is *Introductory Probability and Statistics Using R* by *G. Jay Kerns*. The latter book is developed as an open source project and can be downloaded from `http://ipsur.org/`.

To keep up-to-date information on what happens in the R community, we highly recommend frequent visits to Tal Galili's `r-bloggers.com`. This website collects a large amount of R related blogs in a convenient newspaper-like layout. Subscribing with an RSS reader for smartphone or PC is also possible.

Summary

In this chapter we emphasized the importance of making your analyses reproducible and introduced the concepts of reproducible research and the compendium. How to install R and RStudio in several environments was shown. RStudio supports the concept of a compendium through projects, and if you followed the first session carefully, you have learned to read, alter, and store a simple CSV file, perform some simple analyses, and make a simple plot and generate an HTML report automatically that you can share with your coworkers.

In the next chapter we will take a deeper dive into writing scripts with RStudio.

2

Writing R Scripts and the R Console

In this chapter we will discuss the two panels of RStudio that are used the most—the console and the source editor. Additionally we discuss the history panel.

Moving around RStudio

The features that we will discuss in this chapter are spread across the four main panels of RStudio. Most panels harbor multiple tabs with different functionalities. The main panels shown in the following figure (in clockwise order) are as follows:

- The **source editor** and **data viewer** panel: This panel can harbor a variable number of tabs, each containing an open (source) file or a view of a data.frame

- The **command history** and **workspace browser**: When working with RStudio projects, a tab for version control features can be added

- The **R console**: This panel helps in working directly with R. It has no separate tabs

- The **file, help, package, and plots panel**: This panel is used for browsing files, viewing help, searching, and package (un)loading and installation

The 4 RStudio Panels

Each tab in each panel has its own set of menu items, relevant for the content of that tab.

Every panel has a maximize/minimize button at the top right-hand side. When maximized or minimized, the respective button changes into a restore icon that allows you to restore the panel to its previous size. Panels can be resized horizontally or vertically with the mouse. At the time of writing, diagonal resizing is not possible. The order and content of panels in RStudio can be customized. Go to **Tools** | **Options** | **Pane Layout** to alter the content of each quadrant.

How to change panels?

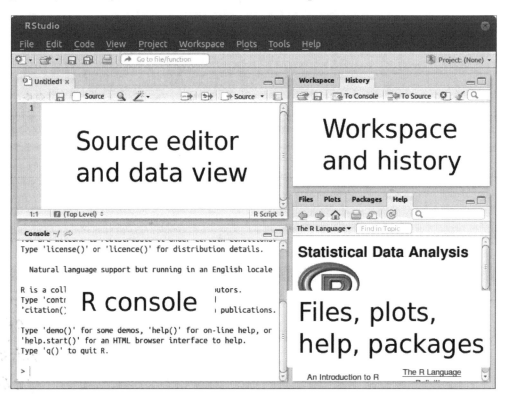

Keyboard shortcuts to move around RStudio

Besides the usual point-and-click way to activate the various panels, there are handy keyboard shortcuts that allow you to move around without taking your hands from the keyboard. Each shortcut is a *Ctrl+<number>* combination and works independently of the current focus. The shortcuts are the same for Linux, Mac, and Windows.

The most important shortcuts to remember are *Ctrl+1* to move to the source editor and *Ctrl+2* to move to the console. The following is a table with every shortcut:

Numbers for shortcuts	Focus
1	Source editor
2	Console
3	Workspace browser
4	History editor
5	File browser
6	Plots area
7	Packages
8	Help
9	Git/SVN version control

Cntrl + Number Shortcuts

You can print all of RStudio's shortcuts by going to **Help | Keyboard Shortcuts | Print**

Features of the R console

We will now talk about various features of the R console in this section.

Executing commands

The most direct way to work with R is by entering commands straight in the console. When RStudio is started for the first time, its interface to the R console is on the left-hand side. The console window has three buttons on its top bar. On the right-hand side, there are two buttons that minimize or maximize the command window. On the left-hand side, just after the word **Console**, the current working directory is shown. On the right-hand side is an arrow that, when clicked, opens the file browser on the right-hand side to view RStudio's current working directory.

```
Console ~/
> 1 + 1
[1] 2
> |
```

To execute a command from the console, type it after the prompt (the > symbol) and press *Enter*. The command is sent to the R engine, executed, and printed back to the screen in a different color. This is the first example of what is called **syntax highlighting** to which we will return extensively in the next subsection. Note that the result is preceded by a [1]. Recall that in R the basic data type is a vector of values of the same type. In the previous screenshot, the [1] indicates that the answer 2 is the first element of the result vector. If the result is a longer vector, each printed line of results starts with a number between brackets, indicating the position of the next value. As a demonstration, generate a vector v by entering the following command:

```
v <- seq(1,100,by=2)
```

This shows the result type v. Press *Enter*. Depending on the width of your window, the resulting vector of 50 elements is shown over one or more lines. In the following example, the window is just wide enough to show 25 elements on one line, so element number 26 starts on the second line.

```
Console ~/
> v <- seq(1,100,by=2)
> v
 [1]  1  3  5  7  9 11 13 15 17 19 21 23 25 27 29 31 33 35 37 39 41 43 45 47 49
[26] 51 53 55 57 59 61 63 65 67 69 71 73 75 77 79 81 83 85 87 89 91 93 95 97 99
>
```

In some cases it is convenient to break a command over multiple lines; for example, when typing a vector explicitly. The R console is able to recognize when a command is not finished and precedes a continuing command with a + sign.

```
Console ~/
> fruit <- c(
+ "apple",
+ "banana",
+ "pear")
>
```

When you happen to get stuck in an unfinished command, you can always press *Esc* to exit.

Command history

Analyzing data by typing commands at the console is not really a reproducible research. However, RStudio offers three ways to retrieve and restore all the commands that you entered.

The first is by scrolling through your commands by hitting the up or down arrow keys, when in the console. Previous commands are shown on the command line one by one. Press *Enter* to execute the current command or *Esc* to return to an empty line.

The second way to scroll through your command history is to press *Ctrl+up*. This opens a popup screen showing previously given commands. You can select a command with the up and down keys or by clicking on them with the mouse. Press *Enter* to copy the selected command to the console, and hit *Enter* again to execute it.

```
1+1
v <- seq(1,100,by=2)
v
fruit <- c(
"apple",
"banana",
"pear")
>
```

The third and the most extensive way to inspect or alter the command history is by using the command history panel. The command history panel is situated in the top right-hand side panel, under the second tab. You can activate it by pressing *Ctrl+4*.

```
Workspace    History

      To Console    To Source

1+1
seq(from=1,to=100,by=2)
v
fruit <- c(
"apple",
"banana",
"pear")
```

The panel allows you to scroll through all the commands that you issued at the command line, including the ones that were given by executing them from the source editor (to be discussed in the next section). After pointing focus to the command history panel, commands can be selected by clicking on them, or scrolling through them with the up and down arrow keys. Multiple lines can be selected by holding *Shift* while clicking on the lines or by holding the *Shift* key while pressing the up and down arrow keys. The search box on the right-hand side allows for searching through the commands. The search encompasses commands given in the current session as well as the commands from past sessions or from other projects.

Commands can be re-executed by selecting them and pressing *Enter*, or by clicking the **To Console** button at the top of the panel. The commands will be copied to the console, executed, and then focus is set to the console.

Commands can be deleted from the history by pressing the **Delete** button (with the white cross in the red circle) at the top of the panel. Alternatively, the entire history may be deleted by pressing the broom button next to it.

The entire command history can be saved by clicking on the **Save** button (with the image of the blue floppy disk) at the top of the panel. The commands are stored with the extension .Rhistory. In the spirit of openness, this file is a simple text file with R commands. So even if you uninstall RStudio, your command history is available to be edited with any text editor, or to be sourced by R. Previously saved command histories can be loaded using the **load history** button (with the folder icon) on the left-hand side.

Loading and saving command histories is not the recommended way to make your analyses reproducible. When working in the console, one typically repeats or alters commands on-the-fly, making a command line history difficult to read. If you performed an analysis that you want to reproduce, there is a better way to do so: by saving it as a source file.

Selected commands can be copied to a source file by clicking on the **To Source** button at the top of the history panel. If no source file was open yet, a new one will be opened for you. This way you may edit the commands into a real script and store them as a .R file, which is usual for analyses automation.

Your history file typically contains many copies of a command. RStudio can remove all duplicated history entries automatically. This can be set in **Tools** | **Options** | **R General**.

Command completion

Command completion is arguably the most important feature that RStudio offers. It is a feature that makes working with the command line a much more productive and enjoyable experience. Command completion is also something you will probably use more than any other functionality, so it is a good idea to familiarize yourself with RStudio's completion features.

Activating command completion is very easy—just type the beginning of what you aim to type and hit *Tab*. RStudio can complete functions and function arguments, objects in the R environment, and filenames (strings). Finally, there is bracket completion, which is performed automatically without pressing *Tab*. Each completion feature is discussed separately in the following section.

We note that many of the command completion features will also work in R's native environment. However the use of pop-up menus, help integration, and bracket completion implemented by RStudio make *Tab* completion even more user-friendly.

Completion of functions and arguments

It is easy to mistype a function name or argument. Tab completion allows you to forget most of a function's name, and most of its arguments. Let's get started right away with an example.

Type s in the console and hit *Tab*. After pressing *Tab*, a pop-up menu shows completion options.

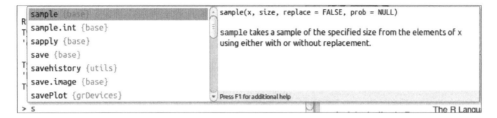

1. RStudio shows a pop-up menu with possible completion options that may include variables from the workspace or names of (possibly self-defined) functions. You can scroll through the options using the up and down arrow keys. Pressing *Tab* again (or *Enter* or *Right*) completes the command and closes the pop-up screen.

2. Behind the function name in the pop-up menu, the name of the package containing the function is displayed. Alongside the list is the **Description** and **Usage** portion of the R help file that comes along with the function. Pressing *F1* opens the whole help file for that function in RStudio's help browser.

3. Once a function name is completed, type an opening bracket "(" and hit *Tab*. RStudio opens a popup with the function arguments and their descriptions from the function's help file. Pressing *Tab* (or *Enter* or right arrow key) copies the selected argument and equals symbol to the command line and closes the popup.

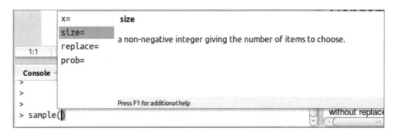

Object completion

The *Tab* completion functionality attempts to complete a non-finished command in any way possible, including names of objects and functions defined by the user in R's workspace. Moreover, for objects that allow R's dollar operator, tab expansion of subobjects is available as well. The most important and useful examples thereof are data.frame and list objects, as it is very common to make typing errors in names of data.frames. As an example, load the iris dataset by typing the following in the console:

```
data(iris)
```

To select a column, type iris$ and hit *Tab*. A popup with a list of columns in the iris data.frame appears for selection.

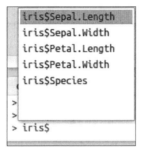

 For the advanced user, completion using the *Tab* key also works for instances of self-defined S4 objects for which the dollar operator has been overloaded.

Completion of filenames

Entering long path and filenames can be a nuisance. Fortunately, RStudio also completes strings into filenames. To try this, just enter a single or double quote at the command line and hit *Tab*. A popup with file and directory names in RStudio's current working directory is shown. For partially completed strings, completions are suggested from the partially completed path in the string. If you are working in an RStudio project, the completion assumes that paths are relative to the project directory.

It is a good idea to use paths relative to your project directory, as it allows you to effortlessly move your whole project.

The previous screenshot shows the popup after typing "/ *Tab* (quote forward slash *Tab*) on an Ubuntu system, showing the root directory structure.

> Recall that R expects a forward slash "/" to indicate levels in a directory structure. As a mnemonic, you may think of the "address" of your file as a sort of web address (URL) that also uses forward slashes. Forward slashes are also common in Unix-like systems and Mac OS X (which is Unix-like at its core). Alternatively, under Windows, one forward slash may be replaced by two backslashes "\\".

Bracket and quote completion

It is an easily and frequently made mistake to forget closing the brackets, especially when several nested commands are used. RStudio automatically completes round, square, and curly brackets with the closing bracket as soon as the opening bracket is typed. The cursor is immediately placed between the brackets. For single and double quotes, RStudio has the same behavior. When an opening bracket or quote is deleted, the matching closing bracket is deleted as well.

Keyboard shortcuts for the console

Many shortcuts that are common in text editors are supported by RStudio, including *Ctrl*+left/right arrow keys to jump a word, *Shift*+left/right arrow keys for selection and *Home* and *End* to jump to the beginning or end of a line. Below is a table of shortcuts for the R console; some of them will be familiar to users of unix shell systems.

Windows & Linux	Mac	Description
Tab (or *Ctrl*+space)	*Tab* (or *Command*+space)	Command completion
Esc	*Esc*	Interrupt current command
Ctrl+up	*Command*+up	Command history popup
Up/down arrow keys	Up/down arrow keys	Scroll through history
Ctrl+L	*Command*+L	Clear console

There are many more keyboard shortcuts, some of them for actions that are probably rarely performed, such as copying (yanking) a line up to the cursor position (*Ctrl + U*). Once you've familiarized yourself with the shortcuts in the previous table, it is advisable to browse through the list of shortcuts (**Help | Keyboard shortcuts**) to see if there are more shortcuts that are useful to you.

Features of the source editor

The most important panel in RStudio is the source editing panel. This is where you write your R scripts and probably spend most of your time working on the project. It has several features that make writing R scripts in RStudio much more comfortable than most other editors. The editor panel of RStudio supports editing several file formats such as HTML, Sweave, Markdown, C, C++, and JavaScript files. In this chapter we will discuss editing R scripts, leaving features for some of the other languages to *Chapter 5, Generating reports*.

> Every code completion feature described in the previous section also works in the source editor.
>
> If you're accustomed to the Vi or Vim editor you can let RStudio emulate some of their properties by going to **Tools | Options | Code editing** and selecting **Enable Vim Editing mode**.

A few words on code quality

A development process, either for a software project or when authoring a statistical analysis, is unavoidably comprised of writing, running, and debugging code. This means that you should try to make your code as readable and maintainable as possible. Here we discuss a few of the most well-known ideas that by now are clichés in software engineering but which should definitely be copied by statistical analysts.

A basic rule of thumb is **Don't Repeat Yourself** (**DRY**). As soon as you have to write a line of code two or three times, write a loop or a function.

> *"Premature optimization is the root of all evil."*

This quote by famous computer scientist Donald Knuth tells you that at least in the beginning of your project, the most important feature is that your code works the way it should, and that you can read and understand it exactly. If you DRY and write functions, it is simple to replace a slow and simple function with a fancy fast one.

The shape of your code should reflect its function. Use indentation to separate blocks such as for-loops and if-then-else statements. RStudio will do this automatically for you, and it is bad practice to ignore or undo the automatic indentation. Use meaningful variable and function names. The name of a variable should reflect the meaning of its content (for example `speed`, `length`). For functions, imperatives describing the action a function carries out are often a good choice (for example `downloadAbalone()`).

In the ideal case, code is understandable without adding comments. However, some complicated pieces of code may need some clarifying remarks. In that case describe *what* the code is aimed to do, not *how* it does it. Realize that just like code, comments have to be maintained. So writing code that is readable without comments can save you a lot of time when fixing bugs or updating your compendium. It is better to have no comments than comments that are wrong.

Editing R scripts

To start a new R script file, click on the new file button (right under the **File** menu, with the green + sign) and select **R Script**.

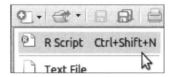

To open an existing file, use the **Open file** button next to the new file button to open the file selection dialog of your operating system. The arrow next to the open file button unfolds a list of recently opened files.

RStudio can open many source files of different programming languages simultaneously. Each file will be opened in a different tab. Filenames appear at the top of the tab. Tabs containing new and unsaved content display the filename in red with an appended asterisk. As different languages require different support features, the menu items of tabs may differ for files. Menus of the editor change depending on the type of file being edited. Here, the menus for R scripts (top) and for Rhtml (bottom) files are shown.

The actions under these buttons can also be found in the **Code** menu. At the bottom left-hand side is the **Jump To** option (showing **Top Level** in the figure) that allows for easy navigation. The bottom right (**R Script**) allows you to set the type of a file and syntax coloring explicitly.

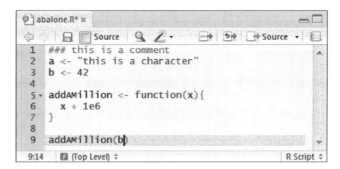

 Files stored with the `.R` or `.r` extension are immediately recognized as R files. Saving a file with this extension will switch on the features supporting R code editing (syntax highlighting, completion, and so on).

Keyboard shortcuts for file navigation

Memorizing the keys for navigation between tabs can be very efficient as navigating between a number of open files occurs more frequently than creating or opening a new file. The shortcut for **Save current document** is very useful to memorize as well.

Windows/Linux	Mac	Description
Ctrl+Shift+N	*Command+Shift+N*	Opens a new R script file*
Ctrl+S	*Command+S*	Saves current document
Ctrl+W	*Command+W*	Closes current document**
Ctrl+O	*Command+O*	Opens document dialog
*Ctrl+Up / Ctr+Alt+*right arrow	*Ctrl+Option+*right arrow	Moves one tab to the right
*Ctrl+Up / Ctr+Alt+*left arrow	*Ctrl+Up / Ctr+Alt+*left arrow	Moves one tab to the left

*Not when connecting to RStudio server on Chrome under Windows

**Not when connecting to RStudio server on Chrome

Keyboard shortcuts for code editing

Most of the common shortcuts supported by many software are also supported by RStudio. These include using *Shift+<arrow>* for selection, *Ctrl+Z* for undo and *Ctrl+Shift+Z* for redo as well as the usual *Ctrl+X/C/V* for cut/copy/paste. Below are some useful shortcuts pertaining more specifically to source code editing.

Windows / Linux	Mac	Description
Ctrl+Shift+C	*Command+Shift+C*	Comment/uncomment selection or current line
Ctrl+I	*Command+I*	Reindent lines or selection
Ctrl+Shift+/	*Command+Shift+/*	Reformat comment
Ctrl+F	*Command+F*	Find and replace
Ctrl+Shift+F	*Ctrl+Shift+F*	Find and replace in multiple files.
Alt+-	*Option+-*	Insert <- (assignment operator)

Syntax highlighting

A basic but important feature of a script editor is syntax highlighting. RStudio automatically colors your R scripts according to the different parts of the R language. This makes it easier to read and edit R code. Syntax highlighting is very helpful in avoiding and detecting typos and syntax errors.

By default, RStudio colors R keywords blue, text strings green, numbers dark blue, and comments dimmed green.

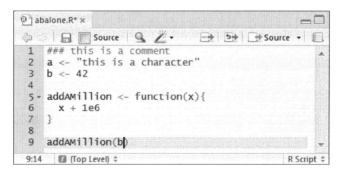

Adjusting the syntax highlighting theme

The style of an editor is to some extent a matter of taste. RStudio allows you to change the font, font size, and coloring scheme used for syntax coloring. The appearance of the editor window can be adjusted in **Tools** | **Options** | **Appearance**. This shows the three options for changing the editor window.

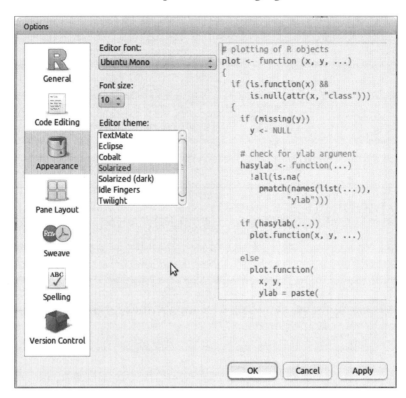

You can change the default font and font size to your liking.

 A fixed-width or monospaced font is preferable because it helps you to structure and indent your code better. All fonts in RStudio are monospaced.

RStudio has several color schemes that you can use to alter the appearance of the source code editor. The color schemes are all inspired by the colors used in other popular editors:

* Textmate
* Eclipse

- Cobalt
- Solarized
- Solarized (dark)
- Idle Fingers
- Twilight
- Tomorrow

Indenting code

When writing R code in the script editor, RStudio automatically indents your code, which results in better structured and more readable code. RStudio does not change the indentation of an existing R script. A script can be re-indented by RStudio by selecting the code and choosing **Code | Reindent** (*Ctrl + I*).

Commenting code

Often during the development of scripts, it can be useful to comment and uncomment lines of code. In RStudio this can be done by selecting code and choosing **Code | Comment/Uncomment** lines (*Ctrl+Shift+C*). Note that activating and deactivating code with comments should not be part of your final work flow — it makes your actions non-reproducible. A better option is to split the code in functions and/or multiple files.

In more mature scripts it is good practice to add comments that explain parts of your code. Editing these descriptions can result in very long comment lines. RStudio can reformat comment lines with *Ctrl+Shift+/*.

> Do not reformat comments on commented code, as the inserted newline characters may break or change the working of your code after you uncomment it.

Find and replace

RStudio offers basic find-and-replace functionality. *Ctrl+F* allows you to search for a text string within the current open document. Typing the string and hitting *Enter* gives you the first occurrence of the text.

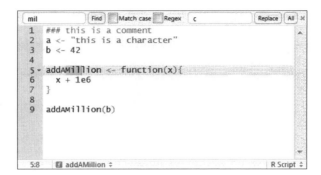

By default searching for the texts is case insensitive, but this can be changed by selecting **Match Case**. It is also possible to use regular expressions (Regex) for searching and replacing your texts.

 Find and replace using Regex is similar to the gsub function in R with perl=TRUE.

With *Ctrl+Shift+F* it is possible to search in multiple files. By default RStudio searches in the current working directory and its subdirectories, but this can be specified.

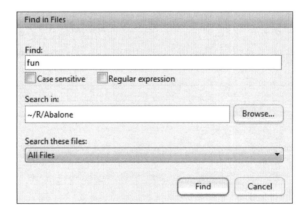

Searching in multiple files results in an extra tab in the console panel named **Find in Files**. This panel lists all the occurrences of the search string. Clicking on an occurrence opens the file at the right location in the script editor.

Folding, sectioning, and navigation

For easy editing and code inspection, the appearance of code in the editor can be customized. Code folding allows you to temporarily hide user-defined sections or indented blocks (functions, loops, and so on). RStudio also offers shortcuts and menus that allow for quick navigation between blocks and sections.

Code folding

Long scripts with many blocks of code can be hard to read. Often this is an indication that the script should be split into multiple files, but alternatively RStudio has a code folding feature that allows you to collapse blocks of code. All the blocks with curly brackets ({}) and code sections (see the following code snippets) can be folded. All foldable code is preceded with a small triangle. Clicking on the triangle collapses or expands a code block. That a block of code is collapsed can also be seen in the gap of line numbers. Here, the folded/collapsed function, the body of the function at line 5, is collapsed:

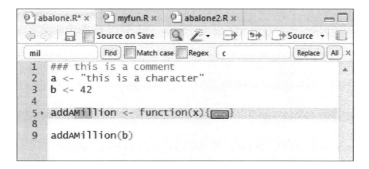

Keyboard shortcuts for code folding

Windows / Linux	Mac	Description
Alt+L	*Alt+L*	Folds selection
Shift+Alt+L	*Shift+Alt+L*	Unfolds selection
Alt+A	*Alt+A*	Folds all
Shift+Alt+A	*Shift+Alt+A*	Unfolds all

Code navigation

RStudio has lots of smart code navigation that can make code editing faster. It is of great benefit to learn some of these tricks, especially if you're develop large or numerous R scripts.

RStudio allows to go to a specific line number (*Ctrl + G*), but as line numbers are shown, you won't use this feature is a lot.

With **Code | Jump To...** (*Alt+Shift+J*) it is possible to jump to functions and code sections within the current file. RStudio shows the available destinations at the bottom of the window. A related navigation feature is hitting the *F2* key by selecting the name of a function. RStudio will open up the file with the function definition. This even works for functions from base R and R extension packages.

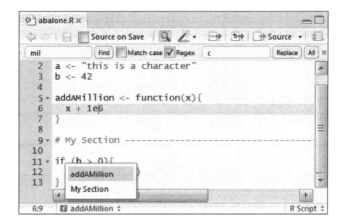

 Functions definitions without curly braces (often used for simple one-line function definitions) will not be found by the jump-to function.

Even more useful is the **Code/Go to File/Function...** (*Ctrl+.*) option. It helps to quickly locate and load functions in your script files. RStudio will show all the available functions and files in the current working directory and its subdirectories that start with the characters you type. Behind function names is the script file where it is located.

Go to File/Function shows the location of functions and files starting with "a".

Selecting one of the listed functions opens the file at the right location.

When writing multiple R scripts simultaneously and jumping between files, it is easy to lose track of changes. RStudio allows you to navigate between files using **Back** (*Ctrl+F9*) and **Forward** (*Ctrl+F10*). RStudio remembers the positions where edits were made and facilitates jumping between them.

Keyboard shortcuts for code navigation

Windows/Linux	Mac	Description
Alt+Shift+J	*Alt+Shift+J*	Jump to function definition (user defined)
Ctrl+.	*Ctrl+.*	Go to **File/Function**
F2	*F2*	Show function definition
Ctrl+F9	*Ctrl+F9*	Back
Ctrl+F10	*Ctrl+F10*	Forward

Code sections

Code sections are not an R, but an RStudio feature. You can structure your R code by partitioning your scripts into sections. Sections are still valid R, because they are implemented as a comment with a special syntax.

The syntax for a section is as follows:

```
# <sectionname> ---
```

Here `<sectionname>` is the name that you want to assign to a section. A section can also be inserted from the RStudio menu: **Code | Insert Section** (*Ctrl + Shift + R*). RStudio will ask you to name your section and insert the comment with the section name.

Code section "My Section"

Note that the **Jump to** button in the editor window (bottom left-hand side) now contains the name of the section.

In RStudio you can use sections to jump to parts of your code or to fold/unfold your code.

Code execution

There are several ways to execute code in the script editing window. Most of them literally copy the lines with R script to the console window and execute them.

To execute the current line or selection use *Ctrl+Enter*. The previous command can be rerun using *Ctrl+Shift+P*.

> Code completion of your code in the editor window will only work if the objects are available in your workspace. Make sure that you execute the assignment of objects in the editor.

Executing a script file line by line is tedious. So RStudio makes it easy to execute (or source) all the lines of a script file with *Ctrl+Shift+Enter*. This will copy all the lines to the console and execute them. The output of the script is printed in the console windows. Note that RStudio treats the execution of all the lines as one statement.

It is also possible to source the current file without printing statements in the console. This can be done with *Ctrl+Shift+S*. RStudio makes this even easier with the **Source on Save** option that is on top of the editing window. Whenever you save your file, it is automatically sourced. This ensures that your workspace always contains the latest version of your objects and functions.

> Don't use **Source on Save** on scripts that take a long time to run. It can be frustrating to wait a long time when changing and saving a file.

Keyboard shortcuts for code execution

Windows / Linux	Mac	Description
Ctrl+Enter	*Command+Enter*	Runs current selection or line
Ctrl+Shift+P	*Command+Shift+P*	Re-runs last executed code
Ctrl+Shift+Enter	*Command+Option+R*	Runs whole current document
Ctrl+Alt+F	*Command+Option+F*	Runs current function definition
Ctrl+Alt+B	*Command+Option+B*	Runs from first to current line
Ctrl+Alt+E	*Command+Option+E*	Runs from current line to end

Summary

This chapter treated the editing and completion features of the console and methods for command history retrieval and storage. Important features of the source code editor were discussed, including code appearance features (highlighting, sectioning, folding), editing features (find/replace, commenting, indentation), and code execution. Some of the more advanced features, such as function extraction and the code viewer have not been discussed here yet. These are left to *Chapter 6, Using RStudio Effectively*.

Now we know how to write scripts in RStudio it is time to see how data can be viewed and plotted.

3
Viewing and Plotting Data

In this chapter we will discuss how to view and edit objects in the workspace. We will also discuss plotting and interactive plot manipulation with RStudio's `manipulate` package.

Viewing data and the object browser

Reviewing your data and other R objects as you develop your analyses is an excellent way to monitor the progress of your work. We will now discuss RStudio's features that allow for the inspection of objects and data.

The panel on the top right-hand side holds the **Workspace** tab. This tab has menu items to load and save workspaces from or to a `.RData` file (R's native format to store data). There is an **Import Dataset** button for convenient loading of ASCII files, as discussed in *Chapter 1, Getting Started*. The **Clear all** button removes all the variables from the current workspace. Finally, the **Refresh** button re-examines the workspace and refreshes the workspace browser.

Buttons of WorkSpace

To show some of the data viewing features, we will use the Abalone project from *Chapter 1, Getting Started*. To open Abalone, navigate to **Projects | Abalone**. If you followed the instructions in *Chapter 1, Getting Started* precisely, there is only the abalone variable. Let's create some extra variables to see how RStudio presents them in the browser.

Type the following commands in an R script and execute them:

```
meanLength <- mean(abalone$Length)
model <- lm(Whole.weight ~ Length + Sex, data=abalone)
x <- 1:3
cv <- function(x, na.rm=FALSE){
  sd(x, na.rm=na.rm)/mean(x, na.rm=na.rm)
}
```

The function `cv` computes the coefficient of the variation. Right now, your workspace browser should look something like the following screenshot:

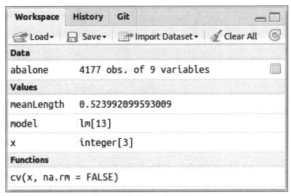

The workspace browser

The workspace browser neatly separates all the objects defined in the workspace in **Data**, **Values** (variables, or objects), and **Functions**. For **Values**, some extra information is shown in the second column, depending on the type of object. For vectors of length one, the value is shown. For all the other objects, the class is shown. The size is indicated between the square brackets. That is, for vectors (and multidimensional arrays) the `length` is shown. For more complex objects, such as the `lm` object in the example, the number of attributes is shown.

Matrix-like objects are gathered under the **Data** section. This includes objects of the class `data.frame`, `matrix`, and two-dimensional `array` objects. The dimension of those objects is shown in the second column. Clicking on the object opens the **Data viewer** tab in the panel on the top left-hand side.

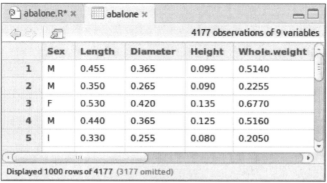

The dataviewer

The data viewer has the following properties:

It shows up to (and including) the first 1000 records and the first 100 variables. When looking for a specific record or subset of records, use R's subsetting capabilities (indexing, the `subset` function) to make a selection before viewing.

The view is not updated when data gets updated. The viewer shows a copy of data at the time the `View` command was issued. You can refresh the view by clicking on the dataset's name in the workspace browser.

Right-clicking on the **Data viewer** tab shows a **Reload** option. However, this reloads the project and not the dataset. See *Chapter 4, Managing R Projects*, for project management.

These features may seem limiting when expecting spreadsheet functionality. However, remember that manually adapting data is not reproducible if it is not logged appropriately. Having said that, data editing is a feature that has been requested by several users on RStudio's forum and such features may be added in the future.

Clicking on an item under **Values** or **Functions** is equivalent to typing `fix(<name>)` in the console. RStudio opens a simple text editor, allowing you to alter the content of the object. However we strongly advise against this practice, as there is no way to easily record such changes. For example, you could alter the content of the `lm` object of the example we just saw, in the workspace. However, you will not be able to re-create this object by re-running the script we just wrote.

According to some discussions on RStudio's forum, the workspace browser is up for some major improvements in the near future, so keep your eyes open for updates.

Plotting

Plotting is an essential need when analyzing data. One of the major reasons for developing R was to enable users to create graphics and charts easily and interactively.

Graphs are also useful as the result of the data analysis. Graphics can be an excellent way of communicating your result. R makes it possible to create high resolution graphics that can be used in scientific publications. RStudio includes several utilities that make both uses a bit easier. It has a specific plots panel that can be found at the bottom right-hand side of your RStudio window.

In a normal R session, all the graphics are rendered in a new graphics device (window). In RStudio, on the contrary, all graphics are by default rendered in the plots panel. This is an improvement upon normal R where a plot command opens up a new window and the command window loses its focus. In RStudio the plot generation does not interrupt the flow of analysis. If needed it is possible to enlarge the plot window and zoom in, but RStudio does not enforce it.

Buttons of the plot panel

It is helpful to know that the plots panel in RStudio does not store the generated plots, but the actual R command that generates them. This makes it possible to generate the plot at different resolutions (aka zooming) or to export the plot to different formats. Let's illustrate the plots panel with the following example. We will use the data example from *Chapter 1, Getting Started*.

Type the following command to generate a scatter plot in the plots panel (*Ctrl+6*):

```
library(ggplot2)
qplot(x=Rings, y=Length, data=abalone)
```

Zoom

The **Zoom** button opens up a new window with a larger version of the current plot. Notice that RStudio redraws the plot at a higher resolution. Whenever the **Zoom** window is resized, the plot is regenerated.

 Right-clicking on the **Zoom** window reveals a menu with the options to save the image. In our experience it is a better option to use the export facility for saving images.

Export

The plot panel allows you to export the current plot to different formats, which can be very helpful. Note that the current export facility is a manual action. Unfortunately in RStudio version 0.97, it is not possible to see the resulting R command that generates the export, which makes using the export button not reproducible. However, the export functionality can help in determining the right parameters for a scripted export version. We strongly advise you to always script your graphics and use the export facility for finding the right parameters.

The export menu has three options — **Save Plot as Image...**, **Save Plot as PDF...**, or **Copy Plot to Clipboard...**. Choosing **Save Plot as Image** yields the following popup:

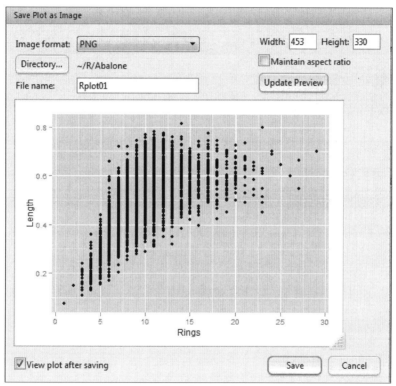

Exporting a plot

The export to image allows exporting to the PNG, JPG, SVG, TIFF, BMP, Postscript, and **Windows Metafile (WMF)** formats. Notice that the screen can be resized by dragging the bottom right-hand side corner. The **Width** and **Height** parameters are automatically adjusted. Copying to the clipboard is similar to exporting to image.

Exporting to PDF generates a one page PDF file with the current plot in landscape or portrait format.

Navigation

The plots panel has several buttons that allow for navigation through previously generated plots.

The R statement generates a box plot of the length of abalone per sex.

```
plot(Length ~ Sex, data=abalone)
```

With the left arrow (*Ctrl+Shift+PgUp*), it is possible to retrieve the previous plot and the right arrow (*Ctrl+Shift+PgDn*) allows you to return to more recents plots. You can remove a plot from plot history by clicking on **Remove current plot**. Hitting the **Clear All** button will remove the complete plotting history.

Interactive plotting with the manipulate package

During exploratory data analysis, it is often useful to play with the parameters of a graphic. This can be done, of course, in the R console by repeatedly executing the same command and changing the graphical parameters. RStudio includes the manipulate package, that facilitates altering parameters of the current plot.

The manipulate function

The most important function of the manipulate package is manipulate. The value of the first argument of the manipulate function must be an expression or function that generates a plot. Various arguments can be added to define custom sliders, buttons, checkboxes, or pickers (drop-down menus) that are to be used in a small user interface (a manipulator) to manipulate a graphic. The following is an example of a manipulator:

```
library(manipulate)

manipulate(
 plot( Length ~ Rings, data=abalone
      , axes = axes
      , cex = cex
      , pch = if(pch) 19 else 1
      )
 , axes = checkbox(TRUE, "Show axes")
 , cex = slider(0, 5, initial = 1, step=0.1, label="Point size")
 , pch = button("Fill points")
)
```

If these statements are executed, a plot is created with a gearbox icon at the top left-hand side. Clicking on the icon opens a small menu box with a checkbox, a slider, and a button. Each time you move the slider or click on a button or checkbox, the variables (pch, cex, and axes) are set to the value chosen in the menu, and the plot is recreated.

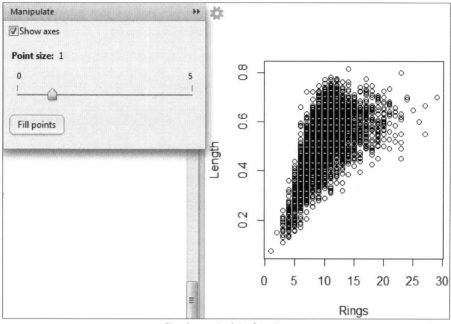

Simple manipulate function

It is possible to have multiple sliders, pickers, and so on, in a single manipulator.

The following is a table showing the possible controls and their outcomes.

Control	Arguments	Result	Use
Button	A label	TRUE from the first click onwards	Sets a logical variable to TRUE
Checkbox	Optionally an initial value and a label	logical	Toggles a logical variable
Slider	**min** and **max** values, optionally an initial value, a label, a stepsize, and a logical (ticks) indicating whether tick marks should be drawn	numeric	Sets a numerical value in a range
Picker	A list of values to choose from, optionally a label and initial value	The chosen value	Selects from a list of options

Using more options of manipulate

After a manipulator is launched it creates the plot with initial values and waits for an action of the user. When one of the controls is altered, the following actions are performed:

- The values returned by the controls are substituted in the corresponding variables
- The expression in the first argument is re-evaluated, causing a new plot

The expression in the first argument need not be a single expression. In fact, the first argument can be a sequence of complex expressions enclosed by curly braces { }. Inside those braces you may use any R command, either plotting or otherwise.

If executing one of the commands takes a long time, for example because it involves computing a complex model, you may store the results for retrieval on reruns after the user controls using `manipulatorSetState` and `manipulatorGetState`.

Here's a simple example:

```
manipulate({
 if (is.null(manipulatorGetState("model"))){
  fit <- lm(Length~Whole.weight, data=abalone)
  manipulatorSetState("model",fit)
  print("hey, I just estimated a model!")
 } else {
  fit <- manipulatorGetState("model")
  print("Now I just retrieved the model from storage")
 }
 plot(abalone$Length, predict(model), col=col)
}
 , col=picker("red","green","blue")
)
```

In the `if` statement of the first line, we check whether the variable `model` was stored before. If it wasn't, `manipulatorGetState` returns NULL. If the variable was not stored before, it is computed with `lm` and stored using `manipulatorSetState`, here under the name `model`. This branch is executed only the first time the expression is evaluated. We've added a `print` command, so the difference between calls will be clearly noticed. If the variable has been stored before (after the first evaluation), it is retrieved using `manipulatorGetState` in the `else` branch. Finally, a plot of original versus predicted values is made. The manipulator allows for choosing the color of points.

There is one more function specific to manipulate, which can be used in the set of expressions passed to manipulate, namely manipulatorMouseclick. This function returns NULL when a plot was made because a menu item was changed, otherwise it returns a list of plotting coordinates in several coordinate systems.

Here is an example where we plot Length against the number of Rings in the abalone dataset and use the mouse to plot an extra cross:

```
manipulate({
  plot(Length~Rings, data=abalone)
  xy <- manipulatorMouseClick()
  if (!is.null(xy)) points(xy$userX, xy$userY, pch = 4)
})
```

In the first line of the expression, the scatterplot is created. Next, manipulatorMouseClick() is called to retrieve the coordinates. The userX and userY coordinates are the ones that can be used directly with the points command.

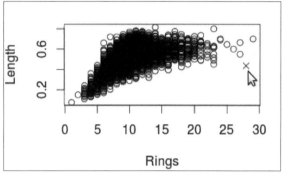

Adding a cross to a plot with a mouse click.

Advanced topic: retrieving plot parameters from manipulate

In this example we will write an interactive plotting function for exploring bivariate plots of any data.frame. We will use manipulate for interactivity but we also want to be able to retrieve the parameters that were set interactively. To achieve this we need some fairly advanced features of R. In particular, we will discuss do.call, sys.call, formula objects, and environment objects. We assume that you are somewhat familiar with R list objects and that you know how to write R functions.

A `formula` object is R's way to express relations between variables. If you ever worked with functions such as `table` or `lm`, you have probably encountered `formula` before. A `formula` always looks something like the following:

```
<dependent variable(s)> ~ <independent variable(s)>
```

A tilde (~) separates the dependent from the independent variables. Functions that take a `formula` as input usually also take a `data` argument as input. For example, to plot the variable `Length` against `Whole.wheight` of the `abalone` dataset, you can use the following command:

```
plot(Length ~ Whole.weight, data=abalone)
```

A `formula` can also be constructed from a `character` object, so the following commands have the same result as the `plot` command mentioned previously:

```
form <- as.formula(paste("Length", "Whole.weight", sep="~"))
plot(x=form, data=abalone)
```

Here, we used the `paste` command to paste the variable names together to a single string representing the formula.

You are probably used to calling functions in the form shown previously. That is, you provide a function name, followed by the arguments between brackets. However, R has another smart way to pass arguments to a function— `do.call`. The function `do.call` takes two arguments—a function, and a `list` of (named) arguments that should be passed to the function. For example, to plot `Length` against `Whole.weight` like in the previous example, we may also use the following statement:

```
do.call(plot, list(x=form, data=abalone))
```

The nice thing about `do.call` is that it allows you to have a function process lists of arguments that are generated automatically.

An R `environment` is very much like a `list`, in the sense that you can store R objects in it. There is one very important difference that we will use here, which is the fact that `environment` objects are reference objects. Usually when you pass a variable to a function, the function may internally overwrite or change that variable without your noticing it, as variables are copied to within the function's workspace. For environments, however, this is not true. Once you create an environment every function that adds, changes, or deletes an object from that environment, changes the original environment. A new environment can be made with `new.env`, and the dollar operator can be used to add or adapt objects. For example:

```
myenv <- new.env()
myenv$x <- 0
```

Use `myenv$x` to view the value of `x` stored in `myenv`. We now write a function that alters the content of an environment.

```
f <- function(e) e$x <- 1
```

Note that `f` does not actually return anything. If you now call `f(myenv)` you will note that `myenv$x` is changed. To understand the difference with a `list`, try the following:

```
L <- list()
L$x <- 0
f(L)
L$x
```

We are now ready to discuss our data manipulation function, shown as follows:

```
dataplot <- function(dat){
 name <- sys.call()[[2]]
 vars <- as.list(names(dat))
 e <- new.env()
 e$data <- name
 manipulate(
   {
     form=as.formula(paste(y,x,sep="~"))
     plot(form, data=dat, main=as.character(name), las=1)
     e$form <- form
   },
   x=do.call(picker, c(vars, initial=vars[1])),
   y=do.call(picker, c(vars, initial=vars[2]))
 )
 invisible(e)
}
```

The input of this function is a `data.frame`. When the function is called, like in the following example, it starts a `manipulate` session and returns an `environment` (stored here in variable `f`) that is going to be used to store everything we need to recreate the plot afterwards:

```
f <- dataplot(abalone)
```

The `manipulate` session allows for choosing an x and a y variable to plot, shown as follows:

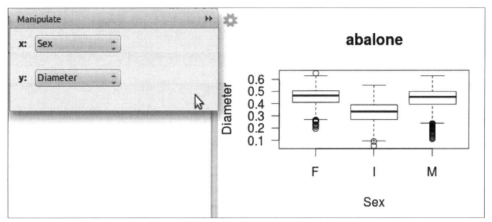

Selecting variables to plot.

In the first statement of the function, we use `sys.call` to ask R what the name of the argument was that was given to the function. Next, the column names of the `data.frame` are stored. These will be used when we create the `pickers` for `manipulate`. Next, an `environment` is created and the variable name of the input data frame is stored in it. Now, the `manipulate` session is launched. The expression it receives will be executed every time you change a setting in the manipulate interface. So we make sure that the variables we want to store are exported to our environment using the `<<-` assignment operator. The x and y pickers for `manipulate` are generated using `do.call`, as we cannot know beforehand which columns are in the input `data.frame`.

After closing the manipulate session you can now replot the plot you made with `manipulate` using `do.call`.

```
do.call(plot, as.list(f) )
```

Or you can do this by passing the individual arguments directly, shown as follows.

```
plot(x=f$form,data=f$data)
```

Summary

In this chapter we discussed several interactive features of RStudio including the workspace browser and the data viewer, and reviewed the functionality of the plot window. Interactive plotting with the `manipulate` package was discussed, including features to store intermediate results and manipulations by mouse clicks. Finally, we discussed an advanced example showing how to extract parameters set in the `manipulate` function automatically.

Now that we've discussed interactive analyses, script writing, and graphical analyses, let's see how we can organize these activities using RStudio's project management features.

4
Managing R Projects

In this chapter, we will cover RStudio projects, RStudio's file manager, introduce version control, and show how to use RStudio's integrated version control features.

R projects

In *Chapter 1, Getting Started*, we introduced the concept of a compendium—the set of scripts and data files that reproduce a statistical analyses as well as the report that is based on it. Managing growing sets of interdependent files, especially when multiple people are working on the same analyses, can be a hassle. RStudio's project management features make things a lot more manageable.

 Always create an RStudio project, even for simple analyses—it makes managing your scripts a lot easier with virtually no extra effort.

Technically, an RStudio project is just a directory with the name of the project and a few files and folders created by RStudio for internal purposes. It typically holds your scripts, data, and reports, which you may manage through RStudio's file manager tab or through your operating system's file manager. The project directory can also contain subdirectories.

When a project is reopened, RStudio opens every file and data view that was open when the project was closed the last time. Moreover, a new R session is started in the project directory, its working directory is set to the project directory, and the history and workspace data are reloaded (if they were saved the last time). This means that when you reopen a project, R will be in (nearly) the exact same state as when you closed it the last time, so you can continue where you left off. A possible exception is when you're using a package that creates objects outside of R's memory space; such objects are obviously not stored in a .Rdata file when R is closed. One example of such a package is lpSolve, which creates a linear program definition for GNU lpSolve outside of R's memory space while the corresponding R object is just a reference to that external object.

Because each project starts a new session, it is also possible to use a `.Rprofile` file in your project's base directory that will be executed when the project is opened.

Creating an R project

To create a new project, click on the **Project** button at the top right above the workspace panel.

Starting a new project

When creating a project, you have the option to start from scratch (**New Directory**), to turn an existing directory into a project managed with RStudio (**Existing Directory**), or to hook up to an existing project and download a project from a repository (version **control**). We will save the latter option for the section on version control.

When a project is created, RStudio creates a text file called `<projectname>.Rproj`, which is used to store the project-specific options such as which LaTeX compiler to use. Although it is a simple text file, you should neither alter its contents by direct editing nor remove it, or RStudio may not recognize the folder as a project anymore. Besides the `<projectname>.Rproj` file, RStudio creates a hidden directory called `.Rproj.user`. This folder is used to store some information between sessions, so your RStudio session looks exactly the way you left it when switching between projects or leaving and restarting RStudio. It is also used to make sure that two different users do not open the same R project at the same time. This wouldn't make sense since each user may have personal pane layout options set and that are not to be shared between collaborators. To collaborate on a project, one usually sets up a (central) repository. That way, each user gets a copy with their own `.Rproj.user` directory. Using version control tools (to be discussed at the end of the chapter), contributions from collaborators can be merged.

 You can easily switch between several projects by clicking on the **Project** button at the top right and choosing from the list of previously opened projects.

Directory structure and file manipulations

For simple projects, a single script file and one data file can be sufficient. But as analyses grow and become more complex, organizing the work in a well-chosen directory structure becomes almost inevitable. A commonly-used subdivision is to put all files of a certain type in the same directory, for example:

- `R`: The directory that holds scripts or files with custom functions

- `data`: All data needed for the analysis

- `doc`: Articles or other documents related to the analyses

- `reports/html/latex`: A directory with generated reports from the analysis

 Use paths relative to your project directory in your scripts. That way, the whole project can be moved or copied and all the scripts will still run.

Navigating directories is done by clicking on a directory name in the file list or on the path shown at the top of the list. The green, angled arrow takes you one step up in the directory tree. To alter a file's name, or to move or delete it, you need to select it first using the checkbox in front of it, before choosing one of the menu items:

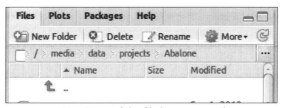

Menu items of the file browser panel

To import files into your project, just copy the file to the project directory or a subdirectory thereof, using your operating system's file browser. RStudio's file browser tab does not support dragging-and-dropping files into its file browser. Instead, the button with three dots at the right of the menu opens a file or folder browser of your operating system.

Data does not necessarily have to be stored in the project directory since R can read data from almost anywhere, including the databases and the web. If your data is not stored under the project directory, it is a good idea to save the references to where the data is stored (paths, filenames, database connection strings) in a single R file that is to be sourced before running the actual analysis.

Version control

In the following sections we will discuss what a version control system is, and demonstrate RStudio's version control capabilities.

Introduction to version control

As a project matures, scripts and reports are often adjusted, rewritten, or discarded altogether. These changes are usually improvements, but it's easy to make a mistake and you may wish to revert changes every now and then. Also, you may want to perform some experiments that require large changes in your scripts. Beginner programmers often solve this by making copies of files with special extensions such as .old or .1. After a while, such solutions usually end up in a kludge of files and directories from which it is hard to obtain the correctly running version, especially when working with many people on a single project. Version control systems are a great way to cope with such a development process.

There are many version control systems available, both proprietary and free, but all systems at least allow you to:

- Store incremental backups of your project and the option to revert to any of them

- Comment the increments so that the development process becomes documented

- Detect when the work of one developer conflicts with another, and mark conflicts in the file

- Branch off a line of development (sequence of increments) that can be integrated with the original branch later

The most important feature that a version control system has to offer is peace of mind. You can safely rewrite your scripts, deleting ugly constructs and replacing them with better ones, knowing that the working code you submitted earlier is safely guarded by the version control system.

Developing a project under version control has the following basic workflow. First you obtain the most recent copy of the project from the version control repository. Next, you work on the project and make changes until, after a while, you commit the changes to the repository, together with a description of your changes.

RStudio integrates with two popular version control systems—Subversion and GIT, where GIT is the default. In fact, RStudio is developed using GIT for version control. The central repository, with the growing code and its revisions, is visible online at `github.com`. The following screenshot shows an example of some commits, showing what developments have taken place. Note that at **Aug 29, 2012**, one of the commits is actually reverted:

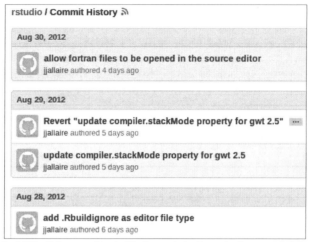

A screenshot of RStudio's commits at github.com/rstudio, note the revert at Aug 29, 2012.

Installing GIT or Subversion

You need to have GIT and/or Subversion installed to be able to use them from RStudio. Both are free and open source tools. Most Linux distributions include a version of GIT and Subversion in their application repositories. For example, under Debian-based distributions such as Ubuntu, open a terminal and type the following statements to install GIT or Subversion:

```
sudo apt-get install git-core
sudo apt-get install subversion
```

Alternatively, use Synaptic or another graphical package manager to install it. For Windows, the authors of RStudio recommend msysGit (`http://msysgit.github.com/`) as the GIT client and SlikSVN for Subversion. The popular TortoiseSVN (`tortoisesvn.net`) is not supported by RStudio since it does not offer a command-line interface that RStudio uses to control the version control system. You can use TortoiseSVN alongside RStudio with no problems, however. For OS X, you can use `GIT-osx-installer` available at `http://code.google.com/p/git-osx-installer`. For OS X version 10.7 and lower, a Subversion client is already installed. For 10.8 and higher, you need to install Xcode and download the command-line tools via Xcode Preferences.

> When you install SlikSVN under Windows, you may need to add the location of `sliksvn.exe` to the `PATH` variable manually. This can be done (in Windows 7 or lower) by navigating to **System settings** | **Advanced** | **Environment variables** | **Path**.

Version control for single-person projects

Although it may at first not be obvious, using a version control system for your own work has its merits. Once you grow accustomed to managing R projects with source control, you'll find it hard to believe how you managed without it. In the following sections, we will demonstrate a simple example, first using GIT and next using Subversion as version control system.

GIT

To demonstrate how to work with a local version control repository, we will work through some examples of our Abalone project. If you don't have those files (anymore), you can download or view them at `https://github.com/rstudiobook/abalone`. When we left the project in *Chapter 1, Getting Started*, we had the following files:

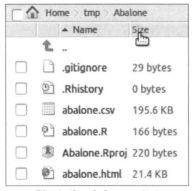

Files in the abalone project

If you set the project up with the **Create a git repository for the project** option checked, there should be a **Git** tab near your workspace browser. If not, you can still create one now by going to **Project** | **Project options** | **Version control** and choosing **Git** as the version control system from the drop-down menu.

Once a repository has been created, working with GIT has the following basic workflow:

1. If necessary, get the latest version of the project from the repository (pull). This is only necessary when collaborating with multiple developers.

2. Do the work—create, delete, move, or alter files.

3. **Stage** changes you want to commit to the repository. That is, you need to tell GIT which of the alterations should make it to the repository.

4. **Commit the staged** changes to the repository.

 If you create a new R project from an existing directory (**Project | New project | Existing directory**) that is already under GIT version control, RStudio will recognize this and show the **Git** tab automatically.

The staging part of the workflow is an important feature that sets GIT apart from Subversion. Staging gives you the freedom to try quick and dirty stuff that you may not want to end up in the repository. It saves you making the famous `<filename>.1` copy, since none of the changes will be submitted as long as you don't stage them. Reverting work that has been staged, but not committed, can be done with the click of a button in RStudio and will be discussed next.

Thus far in our Abalone example, we have only created a repository for GIT. Nothing has been committed to that repository yet, and we first need to decide which files we want to bring under version control. The only files that are directly created by us are `abalone.csv` and `abalone.R`. The `abalone.html` file was generated automatically from our R script when we compiled the notebook. Since this is the output of our script, we do not need to put it under version control. It can be recreated any time we want. The files `.gitignore` and `.Rhistory` are for GIT and RStudio's internal use and do not need to be put under version control right now. In some cases, for example, when working with multiple people on a project, it can still be convenient to bring the `.gitignore` file under version control.

To add files to the version control system, open the **Git** tab, near the **Workspace** panel, and mark **abalone.R** and **abalone.csv** as shown in the following screenshot:

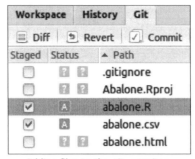

Adding files to the git repository

By marking these files, we tell GIT that the files are staged for submission to the repository. This is indicated by the status icons between the checkmarks and the filenames. The **Status** column has two columns of icons. The right column is used to indicate that GIT has noticed that a file has been changed since its last commit. A question mark means that the file has not been added to version control yet. When you stage a file, the left icon indicates what the committing action will be. In the preceding screenshot, the **A** stands for adding. The following table lists the icon combinations used in GIT's **Status** column.

Icons		Meaning
?	?	File noticed by GIT, but not under version control
A		File is staged for adding to the repository on commit
	M	File is modified, but not staged yet
M		Modification is staged for commit
M	M	A modification was staged, and the file was modified again
	D	File under version control is deleted
D		File deletion is staged for commit to repository
R		File is staged for rename (or move)

The `.gitignore` file tells GIT which files to ignore. You can add files by right-clicking on a file under the **Git** tab and hit **Ignore**. Alternatively, you can edit the `.gitignore` file yourself, using RStudio's text editor.

You can commit the changes to the repository by clicking on the **Commit** button. This will open a window allowing you to review your changes and to add a description of the commit (commit message). In GIT, adding a description comment is obligated.

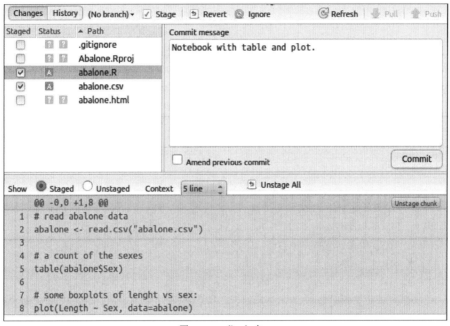

The commit window

Click on **Commit** after adding the comment and then click on **OK** in the following popup to complete your first commit.

Take a look at the preceding screenshot again. The checkbox labeled **Amend previous commit** allows you to overwrite the previous commit with the current commit, when checked. It will be as if the previous commit never occurred—the previous commit and related comments will be lost. It is in general not a good idea to use this technique unless you have a very good reason for it. If you make a mistake in a commit, you can either commit new changes by fixing it or revert it using GIT's command-line interface.

Now, let's see what happens when we move some files around in the project. Using a file manager (RStudio's or your operating system's), add subdirectories called `data` and `R` to your project, and move `abalone.csv` to the `data` directory and `abalone.R` to the `R` directory. Under the **Git** tab, the moved files will be now marked with a red D for deletion—a move means deleting from one place and adding it to another. If you stage the files and folders under the **Git** tab, RStudio shows that the planned action is actually to move the files into the new directories (indicated with an R for rename).

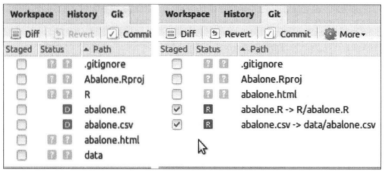

The project directory Git tab before (left) and after (right) staging the new directories and the file moves

 If you move a file with RStudio's file browser that is still open in the editor, the editor will ask you if you want to close the "deleted" file. You can safely confirm since it is deleted from one place, but created at another.

Now commit these changes by clicking on **Commit** and adding a comment, and then close the overview screen.

To show how to revert changes, we are going to make a mistake, stage it, and revert it. Open `R/abalone.R` and change the following line:

```
abalone <- read.csv("abalone.csv")
```

To the following:

```
abalone <- read.csv("WRONGDIR/abalone.csv")
```

Save the file. Note that as soon as you save the file, the letter M (for modified) appears in the **Status** column of the **Git** tab. Now stage the modified file and click on **Commit**. The version control panel opens with a view of the changed lines.

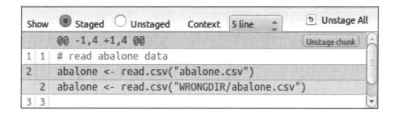

The Diff view shows exactly the changes you made, with the old lines in red and the altered lines in green.

Noting that this is an unwanted change, select the file in the file panel of the version control window and click on **Revert**.

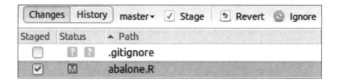

Select a file before committing and revert it.

All changes made to the file will be reverted to the previous commit. Close the commit window and change the line to the following:

```
abalone <- read.csv("data/abalone.csv")
```

And commit the file.

 Always make sure that your main script runs before committing (even when unfinished), especially when working with multiple people on a project.

Now, if you click on **More** and then click on **History** in the **Git** tab, you should see something as shown in the following screenshot:

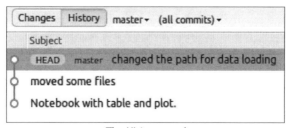

The History panel

In this window, you can browse through the history of your project. On the top right of the **diff** window, there is a **View file** link, allowing you to open past versions of the files under version control. This gives you a simple opportunity to revert changes by copying and pasting lines from a previous version of the file to the one you are currently editing.

GIT is capable of reverting your project to previous commits. This feature is currently not directly available from RStudio. If you need to do this, consult a GIT tutorial and search for "revert". GIT is a very versatile version control system and has many more features that are currently not accessible from RStudio. It is possible to use this functionality directly from GIT; refer to the **Further reading** section in this chapter for some recommendations on GIT documentation.

Subversion

In Subversion, the location of the repository that stores increments of your project is different from the directory where you actually do your work. To create a project under Subversion version control, perform the following steps:

1. Create a new `svn` repository.

    In your operating system's command-line interface, you can do this by typing `svnadmin create <path to projectname>`. A new directory will be created with some `svn`-specific files. You should never alter this directory yourself. It is where Subversion will store incremental versions of your project.

2. In some directory, for example, in `<your home directory>/projects/`, do an `svn` checkout. In your operating system's command-line interface, you can do this by typing `svn checkout file:///<path to projectname>` (notice the triple slash after `file:`).

3. Open RStudio. Go to **Project | Create project... | Existing directory**. Choose the directory that you just checked out from the empty Subversion repository.

4. Or, instead of the last two steps, you can go to **Project | Create project | Version Control | Subversion**. Type `file:///<path to projectname>` in **Repository Url** and RStudio will do the rest for you.

Both for GIT and SVN, there are options to set up repositories online instead of on your local system. Refer to the *Working with a team* section discussed later in this chapter for some suggestions.

We made a fresh empty repository named `abalone`, checked it out with Subversion, and created an RStudio project in the checked-out directory. The RStudio panel now contains an extra tab **SVN**, shown in the following screenshot. We will replay some of the steps of the previous section, but now with Subversion.

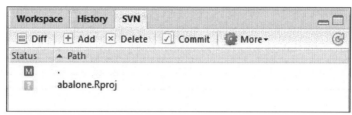

The SVN tab in RStudio

The yellow question mark shows that `abalone.Rproj` is not (yet) in the central repository.

The **SVN** tab of RStudio has a **Status** column containing icons that indicate the status of files with respect to their versions in the central repository. At the moment, there is only the `abalone.Rproj` file, which has not been added to the repository yet, so it is marked with a question mark icon. An overview of SVN status icons is given in the following table:

Icon	Meaning
?	Not in repository
A	Marked for addition to repository
M	Modified or different from repository
!	Deleted in local directory
D	Marked for deletion in repository

To continue with our example, copy `abalone.csv` and `abalone.R` (discussed in *Chapter 1, Getting Started*) into your working directory, or get them from `https://github.com/rstudiobook/abalone`. The files appear under the **SVN** tab and are marked with question marks as well. To tell RStudio which files should be added to the repository, mark the files by selecting them in the **SVN** tab and click on the **Add** button. This will change the question mark icons to A icons. Now, clicking on the **Commit** button brings up the menu shown in the following screenshot:

Commit window for Subversion

To upload your files to the central repository, add a message describing your actions and click on the **Commit** button at the bottom.

Now let's see what happens with SVN when we move some files around. Using a file manager (RStudio's or your operating system's), add two subdirectories to the project directory, one called `data` and one called `R`. Also move `abalone.csv` to the `data` directory and `abalone.R` to the `R` directory. In the **SVN** tab, the moved files are now marked with a purple exclamation mark icon for missing file, and the two newly created directories are marked with a yellow question mark because they are not in the central repository yet. The following screenshot explains this situation:

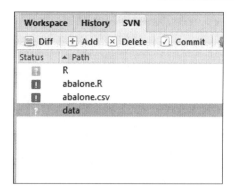

Now, if you select the **R** directory in the **SVN** tab, click on **Add**, and then on **Commit**, the **Commit** window appears as follows:

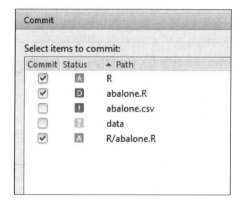

If these changes are to be committed, all of them should be selected. Selecting a directory (such as R) results in the addition of all the files contained in it. Selecting a file marked with an exclamation mark will stage the file for deletion from the central repository. Notice that if you happen to forget to mark a file for deletion that has been moved (for example, abalone.csv), you will end up with two copies of this file—one in the original location and one in the location where you moved it.

To demonstrate how unwanted changes can be reverted, we're going to make a mistake, mark it for addition, and revert it. Open R/abalone.R and change the following line:

```
abalone <- read.csv("abalone.csv")
```

To the following line:

```
abalone <- read.csv("WRONGDIR/abalone.csv")
```

Save the file. Note that as soon as you save the file, the letter **M** (of modified) appears in the **Status** column of the **SVN** tab. To review your exact changes, click on the **Diff** button in the **SVN** tab. You will get a view as shown in the following screenshot:

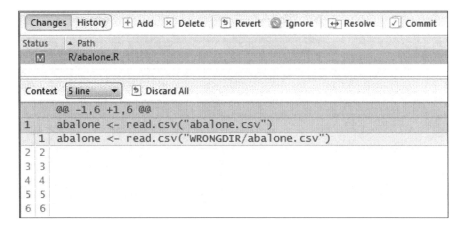

The diff view shows exactly the changes you made, with the old lines in red and the altered lines in green.

Noting that this is an unwanted change, select the file in the file panel of the version control window, and click on **Revert**. SVN will replace the modified file with its older, central copy.

Now change to the following line:

```
abalone <- read.csv("data/abalone.csv")
```

And commit the file.

If you now click on **More** and then click on **History** in the **SVN** tab, you should see something as shown in the following screenshot:

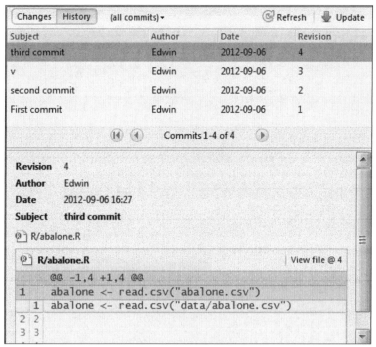

The History windows of SVN

The history of SVN shows all commits to the central repository. Subversion revisions automatically get incremental version numbers. The history also shows who made which commit and when.

Working with a team

Working with a team on a project is almost unthinkable without a version control system. In principle, with GIT it is possible to work without a central repository. However, it is very common to still work with a central repository where collaborators can pull changes from and push their own. There are several online resources where you can host your open source projects free of charge. Popular ones include github (obviously supporting GIT only), code.google.com, and bitbucket. The latter two support GIT as well as Subversion. At the time of writing, bitbucket is the only of these three hosting non-open repositories for free as well.

To start on a project with an online repository, you need to create an account and create a new project at the hosting site. When you create a project, you usually have to choose the version control system you want to use. Once the online repository is created, start RStudio and click on **Project | New project**. Choose **Check out a project from a version control repository**. After choosing the version control system, you will be asked for the URL of your repository and where to store the files on your own computer.

Now, for GIT repositories, the workflow is as follows. To get the updates from your collaborators, pull the latest changes via the **Git** tab menu **More | Pull Branches**. Next, you can do the work, stage files, and commit them with a comment. After the commit, the local copy of the GIT repository is updated. However, to send the same changes to your coworkers, you need to push the latest commits to the central repository via **More | Push Branch**.

For subversion repositories, you need to update your working copy, using **More | Update**. After the work is done, when you commit the changes, they will be immediately uploaded to the central repository.

Further reading

There is much more to be said about version control and we have only covered enough here to get you started with the most common operations. As you grow accustomed with version control, you probably want to start using more features than are currently interfaced through RStudio. The first features to look into are probably branching and merging of development lines and reverting commits. A good online resource for using GIT on the command line is the GIT book (`http://git-scm.com/book`). For Subversion, the SVN book (`http://svnbook.red-bean.com`), which is partly written by some of Subversion's developers comes highly recommended. Both books can be read for free online or ordered as a hard copy.

Summary

In this chapter, we've covered how RStudio projects are built up and gave some tips on how to order the files in them. We've introduced RStudio's file manager and shown how to set up and manage version control for your project through RStudio. Now that we're able to manage projects under version control, let's see how to automate reports with R and RStudio.

Generating Reports

In this chapter, we treat three different ways to produce reports that automatically include the results of an analysis.

A very important feature of reproducible science is generating reports. The main idea of automatic report generation is that the results of analyses are not manually copied to the report. Instead, both the R code and the report's text are combined in one or more plain text files. The report is generated by a tool that executes the chunks of code, captures the results (including figures), and generates the report by weaving the report's text and results together. To achieve this, you need to learn a few special commands, called **markup specifiers**, that tell the report generator which part of your text is R code, and which parts you want in special typesetting such as boldface or italic. There are several markup languages to do this, but the following is a minimal example using the Markdown language:

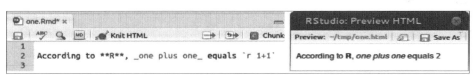

A simple example with Markdown

The left panel shows the plain text file in RStudio's editor and the right panel shows the web page that is generated by clicking on the **Knit HTML** button. The markup specifiers used here are the double asterisks for boldface, single underscores for slanted font, and the backticks for code. By adding an `r` to the first backtick, the report generator executes the code following it.

 To reproduce this example, go to **File** | **New** | **R Markdown**, copy the text as shown in the preceding screenshot, and save as one.Rmd. Next, click on **Knit HTML**.

The Markdown language is one of many markup languages in existence and RStudio supports several of them. RStudio has excellent support for interweaving code with Markdown, HTML, LaTeX, or even in plain comments. We've encountered the latter option already in *Chapter 1, Getting Started*, when we created a notebook straight from R script.

Notebooks are useful to quickly share annotated lines of code or results. There are a few ways to control the layout of a notebook. The Markdown language is easy to learn and has a fair amount of layout options. It also allows you to include equations in the LaTeX format. The HTML option is really only useful if you aim to create a web page. You should know, or be willing to learn HTML to use it. The result of these three methods is always a web page (that is, an HTML file) although this can be exported to PDF.

If you need ultimate control over your document's layout, and if you need features like automated bibliographies and equation numbering, LaTeX is the way to go. With this last option, it is possible to create papers for scientific journals straight from your analysis.

Depending on the chosen system, a text file with a different extension is used as the source file. The following table gives an overview:

Markup system	Input file type	Report file type
Notebook	`.R`	`.html` (via `.md`)
Markdown	`.Rmd`	`.html` (via `.md`)
HTML	`.Rhtml`	`.html`
LaTeX	`.Rnw`	`.pdf` (via `.tex`)

Finally, we note that the interweaving of code and text (often referred to as literate programming) may serve two purposes. The first, described in this chapter, is to generate a data analysis report by executing code to produce the result. The second is to document the code itself, for example, by describing the purpose of a function and all its arguments. The latter purpose will be discussed in the next chapter, where we will discuss the Roxygen2 package for code documentation.

Prerequisites for report generation

For notebooks, R Markdown, and `Rhtml`, RStudio relies on Yihui Xie's `knitr` package for executing code chunks and merging the results. The `knitr` package can be installed via RStudio's **Packages** tab or with the command `install.packages("knitr")`.

For LaTeX/Sweave files, the default is to use R's native Sweave driver. The `knitr` package is easier to use and has more options for fine-tuning, so in the rest of this chapter we assume that `knitr` is always used. To make sure that `knitr` is also used for Sweave files, go to **Tools | Options | Sweave** and choose **knitr** as **Weave Rnw files**. If you're working in an RStudio project, you can set this as a project option as well by navigating to **Project | Project Options | Sweave**. When you work with LaTeX/Sweave, you need to have a working LaTeX distribution installed. Popular distributions are TeXLive for Linux, MikTeX for Windows, and MacTeX for Mac OS X.

Notebook

The easiest way to generate a quick, sharable report straight from your Rscript is by creating a notebook via **File | Notebook**, or by clicking on the **Notebook** button all the way on the top right of the **Rscript** tab (right next to the **Source** button).

Notebook options

RStudio offers three ways to generate a notebook from an Rscript—the simplest are **Default** and **knitr::stitch**. These only differ a little in layout. The **knitr::spin** mode allows you to use the Markdown markup language to specify text layout. The markup options are presented after navigating to **File | Notebook** or after clicking on the **Notebook** button. Under the hood, the **Default** and **knitr::stitch** options use `knitr` to generate a Markdown file which is then directly converted to a web page (HTML file). The **knitr::spin** mode allows for using Markdown commands in your comments and will convert your `.R` file to a `.Rmd` (R Markdown) file before further processing.

In **Default** mode, R code and printed results are rendered to code blocks in a fixed-width font with a different background color. Figures are included in the output and the document is prepended with a title, an optional author name, and the date. The only option to include text in your output is to add it as an R comment (behind the # sign) and it will be rendered as such.

In **knitr::stitch** mode, instead of prepending the report with an author name and date, the report is appended with a call to `Sys.time()` and R's `sessionInfo()`. The latter is useful since it shows the context in which the code was executed including R's version, locale settings, and loaded packages. The result of the **knitr::stitch** mode depends on a template file called `knitr-template.Rnw`, included with the `knitr` package. It is stored in a directory that you can find by typing `system.file('misc',package='knitr')`.

The **knitr::spin** mode allows you to escape from the simple notebook and add text outside of code blocks, using special markup specifiers. In particular, all comment lines that are preceded with #' (hash and single quote) are interpreted as the Markdown text. For example, the following code block:

```
# This is printed as comment in a code block
1 + 1
#' This will be rendered as main text
#' Markdown **specifiers** are also _recognized_
```

Will be rendered in the **knitr::spin** mode as shown in the following screenshot:

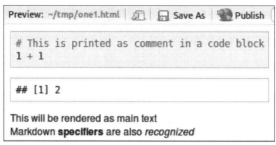

Reading a notebook in the knitr::spin mode allows for escaping to Markdown

The knitr package has several general layout options for included code (that will be discussed in the next section). When generating a notebook in the **knitr::spin** mode, these options can be set by preceding them with a #+ (hash and plus signs). For example, the following code:

```
#' The code below is _not_ evaluated
#+ eval=FALSE
1 + 1
```

Results in the following report:

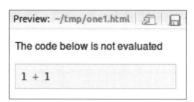

Setting knitr options for a notebook in knitr::spin mode

Although it is convenient to be able to use Markdown commands in the **knitr::spin** mode, once you need such options it is often better to switch to R Markdown completely, as discussed in the next section.

Note that a notebook is a valid R script and can be executed as such. This is in contrast with the other report generation options—those are text files that need knitr or Sweave to be processed.

Publishing a notebook

Notebooks are ideal to share examples or quick results from fairly simple data analyses. Since early 2012, the creators of RStudio offer a website, called RPubs. com, where you can upload your notebooks by clicking on the **Publish** button in the notebook preview window that automatically opens after a notebook has been generated. Do note that this means that results will be available for the world to see, so be careful when using personal or otherwise private data.

R Markdown and Rhtml

Markdown (created by John Gruber and Aaron Swartz) is an easy-to-read and easy-to-write markup language that is designed to make preparing HTML documents (web pages) easier. The Markdown syntax is inspired by how people write plain text e-mails. For example, to emphasize a word in an e-mail, constructs like *emphasized word* or _emphasized word_ are frequently used. Also, people tend to use asterisks or dashes to represent bullet lists in plain text. The idea of Markdown is to treat such constructions as actual markup commands by translating them to equivalent HTML syntax (web page). With Markdown, you can alter the appearance of text by altering its size, typeface, and more. What you cannot do with Markdown, is to alter document properties such as page size, margin sizes, and so on. If you need to control such features, you can consider switching to LaTeX (described in the following section). Alternatively, one can use Max Kuhn's odfWeave package (not supported by RStudio).

With RStudio, you can generate reports with .Rmd or .Rhtml files—in these files you combine R output with Markdown or HTML. Note that RStudio also supports editing plain Markdown (.md) and HTML (.html) files.

Workflow for R Markdown

To create a report with R Markdown, open or start a new .Rmd file (**File** | **New** | **R Markdown**). Note that the .Rmd tab has special menu items.

Click on the **Knit HTML** button (*Ctrl* + *Shift* + *H* or *Command* + *Shift* + *H*) to create and open the report. If a report is already open, it will be updated.

As a first example, let us create a new .Rmd file, empty it, and type:

```
Adding _one and one_ gives '1 + 1'
```

Now click on the **Knit HTML** button. RStudio generates an HTML file and opens it in a viewer. It is important to realize that this HTML file is self-contained. That is, all text and figures are contained in a single file, whereas web pages usually rely on many external references to include pictures, for example. The main advantage is that you can store the HTML file and send it as a single unit by an e-mail.

When a new .Rmd file is created, RStudio opens an example file with a starter guide. If you click on the **MD** button on the left of the **Knit HTML** button, a help file will open showing some of Markdown's syntax. On the right-hand side, there are the **Run**, **Rerun**, and **Chunks** buttons. Since these are present for Rnw/Sweave as well as for Rmd and Rhtml files, they will be discussed separately in the section on code chunks and chunk options.

An extended example

To demonstrate some of the most important capabilities of R Markdown, we will walk step by step through an extensive example. In this example, we'll see how to create a document and section titles, equations, how to include code chunks inline as well as in separate blocks, and how to add links to other documents. We'll also see the first example of code chunk options. You can either type the example in an empty file or pull the example from github by clicking on **Project | New | Version control | Git** and entering https://github.com/rstudiobook/abalone.git.

Also see *Chapter 4, Managing R Projects* on version control. Alternatively, you can copy the preceding URL to your browser and read through the code online.

In this example, we are going to create a report of a simple analysis on the Abalone dataset that we've used throughout the book. We assume that by now you have an RStudio project directory with a subdirectory data that holds the abalone.csv file. See *Chapter 1, Getting Started*, to see how to obtain the file (it is also included in the github repository mentioned in the preceding section).

To start, create a new directory named `Rmd` and a file called `density.Rmd`. In the example, we are going to estimate the "density" (weight per volume) of abalones, by modeling them as rectangular boxes. We start with a title, author name, and date as follows:

```
Estimating Abalone density
==========================
By me, myself, and I. ('r as.character(Sys.Date())')
```

Estimating Abalone density

By me, myself, and I. (2012-09-15)

Here, the double-underlining tells Markdown that the text above it should be treated as the document title (in HTML it will be put between the `<H1></H1>` tag as well as between `<title></title>`). Under the title, we add the author names, and between brackets, the current date as returned by R. This is the first example of inline code. In Markdown, text between single backticks is interpreted and printed as code. By adding an `r` behind the first backtick, we tell `knitr` to replace the R code between backticks with its result.

Next, an introducing section is added.

```
Introduction
------------
If we can estimate the density of _abalones_, we never have to weight
them again!
```

Introduction

If we can estimate the density of *abalones*, we never have to weight them again!

The single underline tells Markdown that the text directly above it is a section heading (`<h2>` in HTML). The text between underscores is typeset in a slanted font.

We continue with the theory section.

```
Theory
------
To estimate the density of _abalones_, we make the model assumption
that they are rectangular boxes with their volume $V$ given as the
product of length, width, and height:
$$V = l\times w\times h.$$
```

```
The density $\rho$ is estimated as from the linear model
$$ m = \rho V, $$
where $m$ is the measured weight of the abalone.
```

Theory

To estimate the density of *abalones*, we make the model assumption that they are rectangular boxes with their volume V given as the product of length, width, and height:

$$V = l \times w \times h.$$

The density ρ is estimated as from the linear model

$$m = \rho V,$$

where m is the measured weight of the abalone.

Here, we've used v (dollar sign) to escape inline to LaTeX mode so the v is printed in an equation font in the result. The difference between the single and double dollar signs to escape to LaTeX mode is that single dollar signs create inline equations while double dollar signs create an equation centered on a separate line.

RStudio uses MathJax to render the equations. That is, the generated web page does not contain the rendered equation itself. Instead, the webpage (HTML) contains a small piece of code that tells your browser to download a library from a MathJax server which is to be used for rendering. It means that this rendering will not work if you happen to work on a closed network without Internet access. In particular, every reader of the document must have Internet access at the time of reading to be able to see the equations in pretty print.

It is possible to install MathJax locally or on a corporate network (`http://www.mathjax.org/download`). After installation, RStudio needs the right hyperlink to MathJax. This link is stored in `<RStudio>/resources/MathJax.html`. Alter the `src` attributes in `MathJax.html` so that it points to your (local) installation of MathJax.

We are now ready to do the actual calculation.

```
Data and calculations
----------------------
'''{r, echo=FALSE, cache=TRUE}
dat <- read.csv("../data/abalone.csv")
dat$V <- dat$Length * dat$Diameter * dat$Height *(20^3)
dat$Whole.weight <- dat.Whole.weight * 200
```

```
model <- lm(Whole.weight ~ V - 1,data=dat)
'''
```

We use the abalone that can be found at the [the UCI machine learning
laboratory](http://archive.ics.uci.edu/ml/datasets/Abalone). This
dataset contains information on 'r nrow(dat)' _abalones_,
including length, diameter, and height. The estimated density is 'r
coefficients(model)' grams per cubic mm with an R-squared value of 'r
summary(model)$r.squared'.

Data and calculations

We use the abalone that can be found at the the UCI machine
learning laboratory. This data set contains information on 4177
abalones,
including length, diameter, and height. The estimated density is
0.5859 grams per cubic cm with an R-squared value of
0.9787.

The three backticks indicate that we are about to start a chunk of code. Between
the curly brackets, chunk options can be set. First, we write r to indicate that we're
dealing with R code here. Next the options echo=FALSE and cache=TRUE are given.
The first option indicates that the code should not be printed in the output. The cache
option tells knitr to calculate the result only when it generates the markdown file
for the first time. The results will be stored for later re-use. Only if you change the
contents of the chunk (or of the chunks it depends upon, discussed in the following
paragraph) between report generation runs, will the chunk be re-run. This can save
a lot of time when developing a report that involves heavy calculations or plots that
take a while to generate. The second triple of backticks indicate that the code chunk
has ended.

In the code chunk itself, we read the data, compute the volume and
estimate the weight per volume with R's default lm function. Note that
the dimensions and weight are scaled. That's because in the original
file, all values are in 200th of a mm and 200th of a gram. Here we scale
it so that the density is computed in g/cm^3.

After the chunk that remains invisible to the reader, we put the main text of the
section, starting with a link to the location of the original file. A link is indicated with
[<link name>](<link address>).

Additionally a few inline R statements are used in the running text.

We conclude the report's final section.

```
Conclusion
----------
This may not be a realistic density, but the fit is pretty good.
```

> **Conclusion**
>
> This may not be a realistic density, but the fit is pretty good.

An introduction to Markdown syntax

A complete description of Markdown is beyond the scope of this book (see the *Further reading* section in this chapter). However, we will introduce some of the most important elements of Markdown, which will get beginner users started and point out the features that are particular to RStudio.

The following table gives a short overview of the Markdown syntax and the corresponding generated HTML:

Markup	HTML
italic	italic
bold	<bold>bold</bold>
# Header	<h1> Header </h1>
Header =======	<h1> Header</h1>
## Header	<h2> Header</h2>
Header ---------	<h2> Header</h2>
### Header	<h3> Header</h3>
[www.rstudio.org] (Rstudio)	<a href="www.rstudio.org">RStudio</a>
* item * item 2	<ul> <li> item </li> <li> item 2 </li> </ul>

Markup	HTML
`| cell | cell |`	`<table><tr>`
	`<td>cell</td>`
	`<td>cell</td>`
	`</tr>`
	`</table>`

Two features that RStudio supports, but that are not part of the original Markdown language, are the inclusion of mathematical equations and typesetting of tables.

Rhtml

If you are accustomed to editing HTML files, you may prefer to embed R code straight into an Rhtml file. An Rhtml file is a valid HTML file with special comment sections signaling that R code follows. The syntax for HTML code chunks looks as follows:

```
<!--begin.rcode
# your R code here
end.Rcode-->
```

The R code must start on a new line and end.Rcode--> must be on a new line as well. Chunk options are given as the `<option>=<value>` pairs, starting with and separated by a comma as in the following example:

```
<!--begin.rcode eval=FALSE
# your R code here
end.Rcode-->
```

It is also possible to use code inline (in the middle of a sentence), using the following syntax:

```
<!-- rinline #your R code here -->
```

Code chunks

In all of the markup systems supported by RStudio, chunks of R code can be embedded and executed. There are many options controlling how the code and its results are shown in the report, how resulting figures should be displayed, and so on.

Chunk syntax and options

Each markup system has its own syntax to distinguish R code from regular text, but in every system it is possible to label code chunks and to pass processing options. Both labeling and optioning are not mandatory and can be left out, so default settings will be used. The following is an overview of the code chunk denominators. You do not have to remember any of them; for each file type, the **Chunks** menu has the **Insert chunk** option.

RMarkdown: .Rmd files

Code chunks are indicated with triple backticks:

```
'''{r <label>, <option>=<value>,... }
# Your R code here
'''
```

Inline code is enclosed in single backticks:

```
'r <R code>'
```

Rhtml: .Rhtml files

Code chunks are indicated as special HTML comment sections:

```
<!--begin.rcode <label>, <option>=<value>,...
# Your R code here
end.rcode-->
```

Inline code is enclosed:

```
<!-- rinline <R code> -->
```

LaTeX: .Rnw files

Code chunks are indicated with the <<>>= @ denominator, following the noweb syntax:

```
<< <label>, <option>=<value>, ... >>=
# Your  R code here
@
```

Inline code is indicated with a pseudo-LaTeX command:

```
\Sexpr{<R code>}
```

The labels allow you to re-use code chunks. For example, in LaTeX syntax you can create a code chunk named `chunk1` and choose not to show it.

```
<<chunk1>>=
1 + 1
@
```

Re-using is as easy as follows:

```
<<chunk1>>=
@
```

Similar syntax applies for `Rhtml` and R Markdown.

Thanks to `knitr`, there are many ways to choose how (the results of) a code chunk is shown in the resulting report. It goes beyond the scope of this book to discuss them all (see the *Further reading* section of this chapter), but we have provided a table with some of the options that we believe are very useful. Fortunately, RStudio knows about the options of `knitr` and their values. Completion is turned on automatically if the filename of the file you're editing is an `.Rmd`, `.Rhtml`, or `.Rnw` file. As soon as you type a comma, a list of options is shown, hit *Tab* to choose an option, and the list of values will be shown.

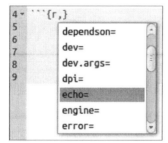 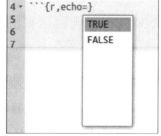

Option completion for code chunk options

The following is a table of basic code chunk options; the default value is shown in brackets:

Option	Description
eval (TRUE)	Whether to run (evaluate) the code in the chunk or not.
echo (TRUE)	Whether to show the code in the report or not.
results ('markup')	<ul><li>'markup': The results are formatted</li><li>'asis': Write results without formatting to output document</li><li>'hide': Do not show results</li></ul>
error (TRUE)	Writes error messages to document.

Option	Description
`warning (TRUE)`	Writes warning messages to document.
`message (TRUE)`	Writes messages to document.
`tidy (TRUE)`	Automatically re-indents the code.
`prompt (FALSE)`	Whether to show the R prompt in the output or not.
`comment ("##")`	The character(s) to print before the chunk's output; use NA to disable.
`size ('normalsize')`	LaTeX only. Sets the chunk's font size relative to the base font of the document. `normalsize` means that the chunk text is of the same size as the main text. There are a fair amount of options, but realistically, `tiny`, `scriptsize`, `small`, and `large` are the only ones you'll ever need. See `?highlight` in the `highlight` package for all the options.
`background ("#F7F7F7")`	Chunk background color. May be specified as hexcode (as in the default) or as a three-vector with values between 0 and 1 indicating red, green, and blue values. Also see `colours()` for R's built-in color specifications (for example, `salmon`).
`cache (TRUE)`	Caches the results so that they do not need to be recalculated each time the report is generated.

It is possible to change the default values in your document by adding a code chunk at the beginning of your document, setting some `knitr` options. For example, to set the comment symbol that prepends all output to '#*', use the following:

```
<<echo=FALSE>>=
opts_chunk$set(comment='#*')
@
```

RStudio's chunk support and keyboard shortcuts

RStudio's chunk menu makes it easy to include a code chunk in your report or to navigate between chunks. For any markup mode (R Markdown, Rhtml, or LaTeX), the editor tab gains a **Chunks** menu.

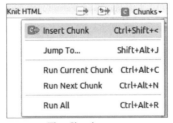

The Chunk menu

The **Chunks** menu allows you to insert chunk syntax for whatever markup system you are working on. You can navigate between chunks, using the **Chunks** menu or by pressing *Ctrl + Alt + J (Command + Option+J)*. If your chunks are labeled, RStudio will show them in a pop-up menu. The chunk in which your cursor currently resides can be executed in RStudio's running R console with *Ctrl + Alt + C (Command + Alt + C)*. The following is a table with some more keyboard shortcuts pertaining to report generation:

Windows and Linux	Mac	Description
Ctrl + Shift + H	*Command + Shift + H*	knit HTML (`.Rmd` or `.Rhtml` only)
Ctrl + Shift + I	*Command + Shift + I*	Compile PDF (`.Rnw` only)
Ctrl + Shift + <	*Command + Shift + <*	Insert chunk
Shift + Alt + J	*Shift + Option + J*	Jump to chunk
Ctrl + Alt + C	*Command + Option + C*	Run chunk
Ctrl + Alt + N	*Command + Option + N*	Run next chunk

LaTeX

The workflow for building a LaTeX-based report is very similar to creating Markdown or HTML reports, but of course you need to know how to work with LaTeX. Create a new `.Rnw` file through **File | New | R Sweave**. RStudio will open a LaTeX template in the article document format. Code chunks are delimited by the `<<>>=@` syntax (see the *Code chunks* section for options) and you can compile the `.Rnw` file to `pdf` via **File | Compile pdf**, by clicking on the PDF menu button on the file editor tab, or by hitting *Ctrl + Shift + I*. Inline R code should be enclosed in the `\Sexp{}` command. Here's a minimal example of a `.Rnw` file and its result:

```
\documentclass{article}
\begin{document}
One plus one according to \texttt{R}:
<<>>=
1+1
@
\end{document}
```

This results in the following `pdf` file:

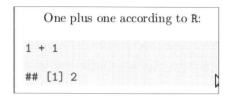

The extensive example given in the section on Markdown is also available in a LaTeX version from the github repository, go to `https://github.com/rstudiobook/abalone.git`.

 When creating slides with the beamer package, use `\begin{frame}[fragile]<your frame code>\end{frame}` to ensure that the code of chunks are correctly included in the verbatim environment.

Working with the `.Rnw` files comes with a bonus—RStudio allows you to navigate between code chunks in the PDF of the source file. To highlight the code section you are currently working on in the PDF viewer, click on the **sync PDF view** to current location button, or press *Ctrl + Click* on the line you want to find in the PDF file.

The Sync pdf view to current location button

This will move the PDF viewer's view window to the current section in the code and highlight a line near the one you selected. Conversely, use *Ctrl* + click in the PDF viewer to navigate back to the source within RStudio.

RStudio does not support command completion for LaTeX. However, under the **TeX** button, some common environments can be inserted with the click of a button.

Further reading

If you want to write reproducible reports, it is nearly inevitable to have to learn at least one markup language. All languages discussed here—Markdown, HTML, and LaTeX—are available in open source. For Markdown, the website of John Gruber (`www.daringfireball.net`) offers a nice overview of the syntax. The Markdown renderer of RStudio is actually based on the `sundown` library of Vincent Martí, which has some extensions. An overview is given at `rstudio.org/docs/r_markdown`. The `knitr` package offers an extensive set of options to control how code chunks are parsed into the final report as well as features such as code externalization that have not been discussed here. Full documentation can be found at Yihui Xie's website, `http://yihui.name/knitr/` (click on the **Options** tab). To learn about LaTeX, the *Not so Short Introduction to LaTeX (Tobias Oetiker et al.)*, included in nearly every LaTeX distribution, is a good place to start. The *Guide to Latex* by *Helmut Kopka* and *Patrick W. Daly* gives a thorough introduction and overview of the system while the massive *The LaTeX Companion (Frank Mittelbach et al.)* is very complete.

Summary

In this chapter, we discussed how R code and plain text can be combined to generate a marked-up report. The markup systems that RStudio supports—Notebooks, Markdown, HTML, and LaTeX—have been discussed with minimal examples and an introduction to code formatting and chunk options was given.

In the next chapter, we will see how RStudio supports writing functions and extension packages for R.

6
Using RStudio Effectively

This chapter discusses function writing and navigation with RStudio and gives a short introduction to authoring R packages. Some background on R functions and package structure will be given as well.

Functions are very much at the heart of the R language. As your knowledge and experience with R matures, you'll notice that functions are not only to be called from the command line or script. They can be passed as arguments to other functions. Hadley Wickham's popular `plyr` package, for instance, makes extensive use of this feature. Writing functions is one of the most important things there is to learn about R, so in the following section, we have given a small introduction to R functions and discussed RStudio's supporting features. After that, we continue with a short introduction to package writing.

Additional features for function writing

Functions are an important tool of programming. Functions allow you to separate a set of operations from the main script and give them a useful name. It also allows you to define variables that are otherwise invisible to the rest of the script; in the language of software developers, this is called **scoping**. Finally, functions can be shared; once you've developed a cool new procedure that takes a data set and creates the most awesome plot, why not write a function for it and share it with your friends?

RStudio has two convenient features for function writing (not discussed earlier in this book) — automatic function extraction and function code retrieval.

Function extraction

RStudio's function extraction feature allows you to select a piece of code and wrap it in a function definition, which can be stored separately for re-use. Here's a simple example. Suppose we've found this procedure that computes one of the roots of a quadratic equation and we've written a small script that calculates it, depending on parameters a, b, and c.

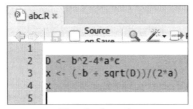

The abc-formula

We first compute the discriminant D, then use it to compute x, and then show x. To create a function out of this code, select the lines of code, click on the magic wand in the editor menu, and click on **Extract Function** (alternatively, hit *Ctrl + Shift + U*, or *Command + Shift + U*, or go to **Code | Extract Function**):

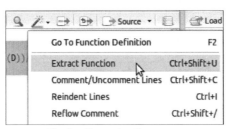

The function extraction menu

Rstudio will ask you for a function name. Here we chose abc. After we click on **OK**, RStudio wraps a function definition around the code and re-indents it. Every variable that was used but not defined in the selected code is made into an argument. Here, these variables are a, b, and c.

```
1
2   abc <- function (b, a, c) {
3       D <- b^2-4*a*c
4       x <- (-b + sqrt(D))/(2*a)
5       x
6   }
```

The resulting function

Note that D and x are not arguments of abc, since RStudio understands they are computed from a, b, and c. To complete the example, store the file as abc.R and open a new script file. Use source('abc.R') to read the function into R. You are now ready to start using your very own function, for example (we use named arguments when calling abc, so their order is unimportant).

```
>
> abc(a=1,b=1,c=-1)
[1] 0.618034
>
```

using your new function

So here's the cool thing about functions; once you've defined them. You only need to know about their name and their arguments, and you can forget about all the complicated stuff that happens inside.

Function navigation

Before we talk about function navigation in RStudio, we will take a little pause and explain a bit more about the nature of R functions. In R, a function is a variable just like any other object stored in R's workspace. That means you may copy it, alter its contents, or delete it as you wish. In the language of software developers, functions are first-class objects. In particular, you can inspect the code of each function, by typing its name in the R console (without the brackets) and press *Enter*. For example, if you've followed the example in the previous section, type abc in the console to see its contents.

```
Console ~/
> abc
function (b, a, c) {
  D <- b^2-4*a*c
  x <- (-b + sqrt(D))/(2*a)
  x
}
```

Now, if we try this with a more complicated function, such as R's built-in summary function, the answer can seem a bit cryptic.

```
Console ~/
> summary
function (object, ...)
UseMethod("summary")
<bytecode: 0x25e3528>
<environment: namespace:base>
```

What R is trying to tell us here is that `summary` is a flexible function. You may feed it objects of various classes, and it will give you a summary for those specific objects. You can recognize such functions by the `UseMethod` keyword in the function's contents. If you've ever worked through an introductory R course, you have probably used `summary` on a `data.frame` or an `lm` object (the result of a linear regression) without even thinking about it. Computer scientists on the other hand, think such behavior is actually quite special. They've even invented a name for it. It is said that `summary` is a **generic** function, with **methods** for all kinds of objects. If you type `methods(summary)` at the R console, you can check for which type of objects the `summary` function will work. We're now ready to return to RStudio's function navigation.

RStudio's function navigation allows you to quickly find out what the internals of a function look like from the R script editor. To view a function's code, type its name in the editor (possibly using *Tab* completion) and hit *F2*. If the function is defined in an opened file, the cursor will jump to the function definition. If the function is defined elsewhere a **Source Viewer** tab is opened (it is indicated with a pair of glasses):

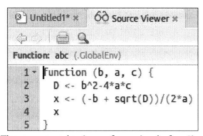

The source code viewer for a simple function

Now, if the function is a generic function and you hit *F2* for it, the source code viewer is also opened, but instead of showing the code, there's a drop-down menu showing a list of each type of object for which the function works. The following is an example of what happens when you use *F2* on the `summary` function:

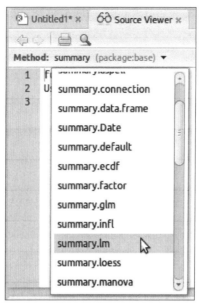

Selecting for which method you want to see the code

Introduction to package writing

In the previous section we saw how you can write a function to be shared with other users. If you want to share a whole bunch of functions with other people, you can consider creating your own R package.

Writing an R extension package has several advantages even if it is not published in a public repository. It allows you to distribute and re-use a set of functions that can be installed on any system that has an R installation. An R package also allows you to hide all sorts of messy functions that are not useful to the user of your package—you can choose which functions are seen by your users and which are not. Functions not seen by the users are for the package's internal use. For example, you could write a function called `discriminant(a,b,c)`, in the example of the previous section that the user of the `abc` function never needs to be aware of.

Packages have a fairly extensive mandatory documentation system that requires that every parameter of every function is described in the reference manual. Optionally, you can include more extensive descriptions and examples. The package system also includes a versioning system, which allows for automatic updating with `update.packages()`.

The details of making and building R packages are described in the *Writing R extensions* manual, which can be found at http://cran.r-project.org/doc/manuals/R-exts.html. This manual is written to be complete and up to date rather than educational and can be daunting at first reading. Fortunately, help is available. Most notably, the packages devtools (Hadley Wickham) and roxygen2 (Hadley Wickham, Peter Danenberg, and Manuel Eugster) help you to author and document your package in a really convenient way. It is entirely possible to develop packages without them, but in the following example, we're making use of these packages so you may want to install them now.

> Since version 0.97, RStudio has support for creating R packages. The Build menu has several package building options and allows for different R project versions that rely on devtools and roxygen2.

Prerequisites

Windows users need to install RTools (http://cran.r-project.org/bin/windows/Rtools/), which contains a comprehensive set of Unix tools for Windows, needed for building and checking R extension packages. When using Fortran code in an R package on Mac OS X you needs to install GFortran (http://cran.r-project.org/bin/macosx/tools).

If you plan to publish your package on CRAN, you will also need to install the latest development version of R. All packages that are uploaded to CRAN are checked against this version and rejected if they generate ERRORS or WARNINGS.

Basic structure and workflow

To create a package, the R functions, their documentation, and the package descriptions should be stored under a specific directory structure. The traditional way to build a package from that is to call R CMD build (Linux/Mac) or R CMD INSTALL --build (Windows) from your operating system's command line on the directory. This then creates a compressed file that can be installed with install.packages() from the R console. To successfully create a package, you need to get a fair amount of settings and files set up in the right place. This is why in the following example, we use devtools and roxygen2 to make life easier for us. RStudio supports both of these packages.

You can follow the example discussed in the following section and recreate the example, or start a new RStudio project from a repository (**New project | Version Control | Git**) with the URL https://github.com/rstudiobook/AbcForR.

Creating the package directory structure

In this example, we are going to develop the abc function, discussed in the previous section, into a package. We first need to set up a directory structure. Fortunately, R contains a utility function that does this for us. Make sure that the abc function is loaded into R's workspace and type the following in the console:

```
package.skeleton("AbcForR", list="abc")
```

Here, the first argument is the name of the package and the second is a list of functions to include. Optionally, you can add a third argument (named path) to tell R where to create the package directory. In this case, we create a package directory under the current working directory. Now create a new RStudio project in the AbcForR directory (**New Project | Existing directory**). Open the DESCRIPTION file and change the title to The abc formula for R. Note that the abcForR/R project directory contains abc.R with our function abc. package.skeleton also creates a man directory for documentation files and a NAMESPACE file. These can be edited manually, but we will use devtools and roxygen2 to generate these files, so they can be deleted.

 Another way to start building a package is to start a special RStudio project. Go to **Project | Create Project... | New Project**. Choose **Package** under the **Type** drop-down menu. When you click on the **Create Project** button, RStudio also executes package.skeleton for you to create the file and directory structure for an empty package.

Documenting functions with Roxygen2

Roxygen2 is an R extension that helps to document functions. The idea is that you add a block of special comments before the function code that describes the function. Roxygen2 recognizes the special block and uses it to generate the .Rd files in your package's man directory, which will ultimately result in your package's HTML help files and reference manual. So here's the advantage; instead of having to maintain both a file with R code and a file with documentation, Roxygen2 allows you to combine everything in a single file that is much easier to maintain and your manual is created automatically. Moreover, RStudio has excellent support for Roxygen2 style documentation.

Roxygen2 works with a special comment syntax #' (hash and single quote) to indicate which part of the comments contain function descriptions. Tags, starting with @, are used to specify the various aspects of documentation. To continue our example, open R/abc.R and add the following comments just above the function code.

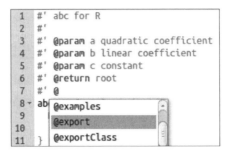

RStudio helps documenting by showing the available tags as soon as you type @. The first line will be the title of the abc function in the reference manual. Next come the @param tags. These are important (and mandatory) since they are used to describe the parameters of the function to the user. Finally, the @export tag tells Roxygen2 that any user who installs and loads this package may use this function. If you leave this tag out, the function will not be exported.

Roxygen2 has many tags allowing you to customize the reference manual. A complete list of tags with explanations can be found by typing ?rd_roclets at the R command line. The following table is an overview of some of the most important ones:

Tag	Documents
@param <name> <description>	Parameter of function, required for each parameter
@return <description>	Return value of function
@export	Exports function (no documentation)
@examples <R code>	Example code demonstrating the function (inline)
@example <path to R file>	Example code demonstrating the function
@note <contents>	Creates a Note section
@section <name> : <contents>	Creates a named section (note the ":")
@references <reference>	Creates a reference to literature

Now, after saving our abc.R file, we could use the roxygenize function on the file abc.R to generate the .Rd file for our package. Could, because we're not actually going to do this ourselves; we're going to let some functions from the devtools package do all the hard work for us, in the next subsection.

Building your package with devtools

The `devtools` package makes developing, documenting, checking, building, and testing an R package a breeze. All `devtools` functions remember the current package you are working on and most functions won't need parameters.

To create the package, we first need to create the documentation files. Simply load the `devtools` package and run `document()`. This will generate the `.Rd` files that will be used by R when the actual package is built.

```
> document()
Loading required package: roxygen2
Loading required package: digest
Updating AbcForR documentation
Updating namespace directives
Writing abc.Rd
```

Creating the .Rd files with the devtools package

Next, run `build()` to create the package. The package is stored one directory above the project directory you are working in. You can now install your package by typing the following in R's console:

```
install.packages("../<your packagefile>")
```

It can now be loaded with library like any other package. The following is a screenshot of the `abc` function's help page:

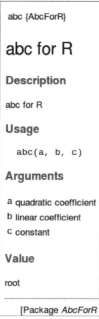

Documentation of the abc function

Developing a package is not usually a matter of write-document-build, like in the example given here. Developing a package usually means lots of writing, loading, testing, and testing iterations of functions and documentation, before the final `build` command is given. In the next subsection, we will discuss a few features of the `devtools` package that make this process easier.

More about the devtools package

The `devtools` package has a number of features that facilitate the many iterations of writing, loading, testing, and debugging functions that you're likely to go through when you're developing a package. Full documentation can, of course, be found in Devtools' help pages, but in our experiences the functions listed in the following table are the ones you will probably use the most:

Function	RStudio shortcut	Description
`load_all()`	*Ctrl + Shift + L* or *Cmd + Shift + L*	Loads (reloads) all functions in your package without actually building it
`document()`		Creates the `.Rd` files from in-code Roxygen2 documentation specification
`install()`	*Ctrl + Shift + B* or *Cmd + Shift + B(*)*	Installs the package straight from source
`check()`	*Ctrl + Shift + E* or *Cmd + Shift + E(*)*	Temporarily installs the package and runs all CRAN tests on it (see the *Publishing your package* section)
`dev_mode()`		Initiate development mode; all installations will go to a temporary library so your normal R installation is not affected Turn off with `dev_mode(on=FALSE)`

(*)These shortcuts do not call Devtools' `install()` or `check()`, but directly execute the equivalent `R CMD INSTALL` or `R CMD CHECK`.

Publishing your package

There are several ways to make your package available to the public. You can post it on a website, put it in an open repository such as `github`, or publish it via a public repository such as CRAN or `omegahat.org`.

Package publishing via github is actually supported by `devtools` — it includes a function called `install_github`, which attempts to install a package straight from the developer's `github` repository. For example, to install the `AbcForR` package from `github`, execute the following command:

```
install_github('AbcForR', 'rstudiobook')
```

Packages submitted to CRAN are thoroughly checked and published only if they are fully documented. If the check or installation process generates errors or warnings, the package will not be accepted. If a note is generated, the CRAN maintainers will ask you to explain why the note is not taken care of, and you will probably have to fix it still.

The CRAN maintainers are doing a great job and their time is scarce, so be sure that your package passes `check()` without any trouble before submitting. Also, do read the CRAN repository policy at `http://cran.r-project.org/web/packages/policies.html` before submitting. You need to agree with these policies when submitting a new package. Once you're ready to submit a package, the release function of the `devtools` package allows you to automatically submit a package to CRAN.

Summary

This chapter discussed function extraction and navigation features of RStudio and gave a little bit of background on R functions. An overview was given showing how functions can be combined in a package, using the `devtools` and `roxygen2` packages.

Index

Thank you for buying
Learning RStudio for R Statistical Computing

About Packt Publishing

Packt, pronounced 'packed', published its first book "*Mastering phpMyAdmin for Effective MySQL Management*" in April 2004 and subsequently continued to specialize in publishing highly focused books on specific technologies and solutions.

Our books and publications share the experiences of your fellow IT professionals in adapting and customizing today's systems, applications, and frameworks. Our solution based books give you the knowledge and power to customize the software and technologies you're using to get the job done. Packt books are more specific and less general than the IT books you have seen in the past. Our unique business model allows us to bring you more focused information, giving you more of what you need to know, and less of what you don't.

Packt is a modern, yet unique publishing company, which focuses on producing quality, cutting-edge books for communities of developers, administrators, and newbies alike. For more information, please visit our website: www.packtpub.com.

About Packt Open Source

In 2010, Packt launched two new brands, Packt Open Source and Packt Enterprise, in order to continue its focus on specialization. This book is part of the Packt Open Source brand, home to books published on software built around Open Source licences, and offering information to anybody from advanced developers to budding web designers. The Open Source brand also runs Packt's Open Source Royalty Scheme, by which Packt gives a royalty to each Open Source project about whose software a book is sold.

Writing for Packt

We welcome all inquiries from people who are interested in authoring. Book proposals should be sent to author@packtpub.com. If your book idea is still at an early stage and you would like to discuss it first before writing a formal book proposal, contact us; one of our commissioning editors will get in touch with you.

We're not just looking for published authors; if you have strong technical skills but no writing experience, our experienced editors can help you develop a writing career, or simply get some additional reward for your expertise.

R Graph Cookbook

ISBN: 978-1-84951-306-7   Paperback: 272 pages

Detailed hands-on recipes for creating the most useful types of graphs in R-starting from the simplest versions to more advanced applications

1. Learn to draw any type of graph or visual data representation in R

2. Filled with practical tips and techniques for creating any type of graph you need; not just theoretical explanations

3. All examples are accompanied with the corresponding graph images, so you know what the results look like

gnuplot Cookbook

ISBN: 978-1-84951-724-9   Paperback: 220 pages

Over 80 recipes to visually explore the full range of features of the world's preeminent open source graphing system

1. See a picture of the graph you want to make and find a ready-to-run script to produce it

2. Working examples of using gnuplot in your own programming language... C, Python, and more

3. Find a problem-solution approach with practical examples enriched with good pictorial illustrations and code

Please check **www.PacktPub.com** for information on our titles

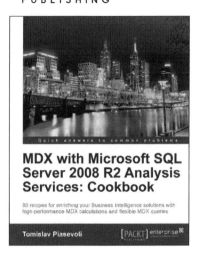

MDX with Microsoft SQL Server 2008 R2 Analysis Services: Cookbook

80 recipes for enriching your Business Intelligence solutions with high-performance MDX calculations and flexible MDX queries

Tomislav Piasevoli   [PACKT] enterprise

MDX with Microsoft SQL Server 2008 R2 Analysis Services Cookbook

ISBN: 978-1-84968-130-8   Paperback: 480 pages

80 recipes for enriching your Business Intelligence solutions with high-preformance MDX calculations and flexible MDX queries

1. Enrich your BI solutions by implementing best practice MDX calculations

2. Master a wide range of time-related, context-aware, and business-related calculations

3. Enhance your solutions by combining MDX with utility dimensions

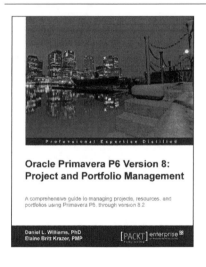

Oracle Primavera P6 Version 8: Project and Portfolio Management

A comprehensive guide to managing projects, resources, and portfolios using Primavera P6, through version 8.2

Daniel L. Williams, PhD
Elaine Britt Krazer, PMP   [PACKT] enterprise

Oracle Primavera P6 Version 8: Project and Portfolio Management

ISBN: 978-1-84968-468-2   Paperback: 348 pages

A comprehensive guide to managing projects, resources, and portfolios using Primavera P6, through version 8.2

1. Get a detailed overview of Oracle Primavera P6 Enterprise Project Portfolio Management.

2. Manage your projects from just anywhere using simple e-mail and the P6 iPhone app.

3. Learn to create a new project in the P6 Professional Client

Please check **www.PacktPub.com** for information on our titles

Made in the USA
Middletown, DE
03 March 2016